ACTION *Is the*
SECRET *to*
ATTRACTION

ACTION *Is the* SECRET *to* ATTRACTION

12 STEPS to Manifest Your Dreams

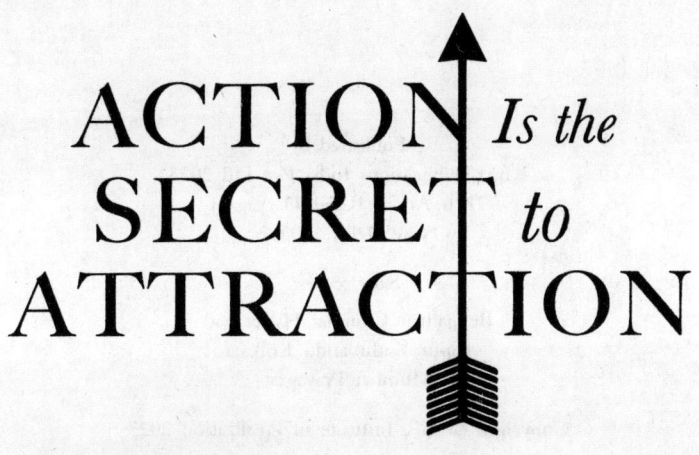

Atman in Ravi

Published by
Rupa Publications India Pvt. Ltd 2025
7/16, Ansari Road, Daryaganj
New Delhi 110002

Sales centres:
Bengaluru Chennai Hyderabad
Jaipur Kathmandu Kolkata
Mumbai Prayagraj

Copyright © AiR Institute of Realization 2025

The views and opinions expressed in this book are the author's own and the facts are as reported by him, which have been verified to the extent possible, and the publishers are not in any way liable for the same.

The publisher has used its best endeavours to ensure that URLs for external websites referred to in this book are correct and active at the time of going to press. However, the publisher has no responsibility for the websites and can make no guarantee that a site will remain live or that the content is or will remain appropriate.

All rights reserved.

No part of this publication may be reproduced, transmitted or stored in a retrieval system, in any form or by any means, electronic, mechanical, photocopying, recording or otherwise, without the prior permission of the publisher.

P-ISBN: 978-93-6156-799-5
E-ISBN: 978-93-6156-331-7

First impression 2025

10 9 8 7 6 5 4 3 2 1

The moral right of the author has been asserted.

Printed in India

This book is sold subject to the condition that it shall not, by way of trade or otherwise, be lent, resold, hired out or otherwise circulated, without the publisher's prior consent, in any form of binding or cover other than that in which it is published.

'The law of attraction says *like attracts like*,
so when you think a thought,
you are also attracting *like* thoughts to you.'

—Rhonda Byrne, *The Secret*

CONTENTS

Preface	ix
Introduction	1
Within the Law of Attraction Is Action	9
Step 1: Discover the Law of Attraction	15
Step 2: Understand the Power of Visualization	25
Step 3: Use the Thought-Chain for Manifestation	35
Step 4: Get into Action, Action, Action	45
Step 5: Activate the Secret Equation: Attraction + Action	59
Step 6: Choose Positive Over Negative through Discrimination	67

Step 7: Be in Consciousness for Purification   75

Step 8: Light the Spark of Illumination
for Realization   85

Step 9: Realize that Twin Karma Decides
Our Destination   95

Step 10: Achieve the Goal of Liberation and
Divine Unification   105

Step 11: Convert Information to a Transformation 115

Step 12: Eliminate Confusion and Get to the
Conclusion   125

Afterword   133

My 'Giving' Journey   137

List of Books by AiR   149

PREFACE

There is a powerful Law called the Law of Attraction.
This Law is visualization; it is manifestation.
But to make Attraction work;
What is the secret equation?
Let us discover it and have a Transformation.

The Law of Attraction is a powerful Universal Law. However, does Attraction work just by attracting our dreams and goals? No! There is a process that makes Attraction work.

After writing over 80 books on the subjects of life, happiness and Enlightenment, I met many people who talked to me about the Law of Attraction. They were enamoured by this powerful phenomenon of visualization and manifestation. When I talked to them about the Law of Action or Karma, they wondered whether it was Attraction or Action that would take them to their destination. So I decided to write a book that guides us to contemplate, introspect and realize the truth. If one looks into the word 'Attraction', one will find the word 'Action' embedded in it. If you remove the word 'Action', there will be no Attraction. Therefore, Attraction is very powerful but it will not lead to manifestation without Action.

Authors and philosophers worldwide have proclaimed that the Law of Attraction can make any dream come true. There is power in visualization. They believe whatever we attract will manifest in our life. No doubt, it will! But think about it. If you lock yourself in your house and keep on attracting and visualizing your dream, do you think that Attraction has a magical force that will make your dream come true? *Unless you take your dreams and put them under some powerful beams, activate them with schemes, and execute the dreams with teams, your dream will not get that gleam called success.* The dreams will just remain dreams. So it is with Attraction. Unless Attraction is backed by Action, we will never reach our destination. I realized this truth after writing five books on Karma, the Law of Action. I realized the truth that Attraction

Preface

will give us direction but Action will take us to our destination. Attraction has the power of visualization but ultimately manifestation depends on Action. Therefore, what is more important—Attraction or Action?

In this book, I will share my personal experience on the power of thought, how thoughts can make us or break us and how we must use the power of Attraction and the Law of Action to reach our ultimate destination. I will share my life experience of how positive thinking transformed my life. I read hundreds of books that said 'think positive'. But how to 'think positive'? I discovered that the mind is nothing but a thought factory. It produces thoughts based on the raw material we feed it. If we feed the mind with PEP, POSITIVE ENERGY POWER, we will automatically think positive. But if we feed the mind with NEP, NEGATIVE ENERGY POISON, then these emotions will create toxic thoughts. I realized that thoughts were the starting point of all achievement and if we attracted the wrong thoughts, whatever Action we performed, would only take us in the wrong direction. Therefore, I discovered the secret equation of Attraction + Action, which I share in this book.

Attraction without Action will create a passion but that passion will not take us to our destination. Action without Attraction will make us work hard but we will not achieve our dreams and goals. Unless we work smart by using our intellect and the power of positive thinking, we will slog like hell but never ring the success bell. I experienced both the Law of Attraction and the Law of Action working in synchronicity in my life. Each would be incomplete without the other. So while I realized how closely Attraction and Action are connected, I ultimately went a step further.

Like everybody else, early in life, I too was chasing success, wealth and fame. I would apply the principles of the Law of Attraction coupled with Action to manifest my material dreams. Little did I realize that I was on the wrong path completely. Why do we seek what we seek? To be happy. But are we really happy? Unfortunately, no. Inspired by my guru, I realized that there was only one way to uninterrupted and seamless peace and bliss. In this book, I will share how I used the power of Attraction through proper discrimination and converted information into a transformation, which led to a life of bliss and joy. What we need is Self-realization. We need to deploy the Law of Attraction and Action, to reach not only some material, worldly destination but also the ultimate destination of life—Enlightenment.

Isn't it ironic that we all want to be happy but in chasing success and achievement, we are unable to reach that state of contentment and fulfilment? We live and we die. We look up at the sky, cry, and question, 'Why?' We don't realize the truth of 'Who am I?' There is no Self-realization. Therefore, we suffer the triple suffering—pain of the body, misery of the mind and agony of the ego. I discovered the power of Attraction and activated the Law of Action and used this combination to reach that state of eternal peace and everlasting happiness.

On my journey, I learnt many things. To start with, I discovered something that surprised me. When I tried to find the mind, I could not find it. This led me to transcend both Attraction and Action to a state of Divine Unification. This is our ultimate goal—To realize we are not the body that does the Action and we are not the mind that is responsible for Attraction. We are the Divine Soul. We need this Self-realization.

This book can transform your life. If you understand how the Law of Attraction works and you look deeper to discover the Law of Action that is embedded in Attraction, you will be able to take charge of your destiny. Just like the seed you plant decides the fruit on the tree, the deed you plant will decide your destiny. But what the deed is will depend upon what you think and visualize. This is what you will ultimately realize. Therefore, let us learn to combine Attraction and Action and reach our destination. Let us discover the power of the equation — Attraction + Action. This book will reveal a step-by-step method, which I not only discovered but also executed in my life to make every dream come true. This book will not stop at just Attraction and Action but it will take you to Self-realization which is our ultimate destination.

'The law of attraction states that whatever you focus on, think about, read about, and talk about intensely, you're going to attract more of into your life.'

—JACK CANFIELD

INTRODUCTION

This is just the introduction,
But it will take you to your Destination,
Provided you use both Attraction and Action,
With discrimination that will create Illumination.

How can we make the Law of Attraction work for us? We can make the Law of Attraction work for us by executing the Law of Action, called Karma.

What is Karma, the Law of Action? It is a Universal Law that states, 'As you sow, so shall you reap. What you do will come back to you. What you give is what you get.' It is the Law of Cause and Effect. What goes around, comes around, like a boomerang.

In this book, I will share with you 12 specific steps that will start with Attraction and end with reaching our destination. However, to make anything happen, we have to follow the process. If we deviate from the method, we will be heading in the wrong direction. We cannot blame the Law of Attraction because the Law of Attraction is a Law. It works. However, we are ignorant and because we do not understand how it works, we blame the Law. Whatever is happening, is happening either as per our present actions, which we understand, or it is unfolding as per our past actions that we have either forgotten or actions from our previous lives that we don't understand. Everybody wants happiness. But not everybody realizes the true meaning of happiness. Because we think success is happiness, we don't discover the truth that, in fact, happiness is success. When we use Attraction with discrimination, we will discover the secret of success. What are the 12 steps that will make Attraction work?

~

It all starts with Attraction. The starting point of all achievements is *thought*. Without the right thought, we will never start our journey towards success. Therefore, we must discover the power of the Law of Attraction. This is the first step. But we must not misunderstand it. Attraction by itself will only create a powerful passion.

If we do not light a fire and convert the passion into Action, we should not blame the Law of Attraction because we have not used all the steps of the Law of Attraction, such as Action. Therefore, we cannot reach our destination.

The second step is to take Attraction into passionate visualization. Not only must we think but we must also attract. The power of repetitive thought is phenomenal, whether it is a positive thought that will empower our passion or a toxic thought that will lead us into depression. Therefore, we have to use visualization in the right way.

The third step is to understand the thought-chain and how manifestation happens. Manifestation is not a magic show. Thoughts become feelings and feelings become actions. It is a systematic evolution that starts with a thought and ends with an Action. Therefore, whatever the result is, it is because of the manifestation of our Action and our Attraction. Those who think that visualization and manifestation are a magical force will end up being disappointed.

The fourth step is the most important one. It is the Law of Action. It is the Universal Law that governs everything that happens on Earth. It is the reason why we are born. But not many of us decode the mystery that fills our history. Nothing happens by magic. Everything has a clear logic. Just like the fruits on trees depend on the seeds, our destiny is controlled by our deeds. Unless we discover the Law of Action, the Law of Attraction will be an unfulfilled visualization. This part of the book is the key that will unlock the door to your dreams.

The fifth step is the real secret. It is the equation of Attraction + Action that will result in all manifestations. Just Attraction doesn't work and just Action will get us nowhere. But the combination is a secret equation for success.

The sixth step is how to use the power of discrimination to choose PEP over NEP. We can be glad or we can be sad. We can be positive or we can be negative. Humans are the only ones who have been given the power of intelligence. We are blessed with a fully developed intellect to discriminate and choose. And if we lose this opportunity, we will lose the chance of achieving our ultimate goal. We cannot control thought but we can control our Action by intercepting thought with intellect and discrimination. This will take us forward in our journey of Attraction.

The seventh step is going beyond Attraction and Action. It is the key to reaching our ultimate destination. It is moving from a state of mind to a state of Consciousness, from a state of toxic thoughts to a state of Thoughtlessness. How can we let the process of Attraction and discrimination go through Purification before thoughts are put into Action? If we let toxic thoughts get executed, then we will be full of junk. But if we use discrimination for Purification, we can live blissfully like a monk.

The eighth step is about Illumination and how Attraction and Action are of little meaning unless there is Illumination. The objective of thinking and doing is to attain that ultimate state called Realization. Our first goal is Self-realization and then, God-realization. Unless there is illumination, we will not overcome ignorance and realize the truth about life. Therefore, we must use Attraction followed by Action to attain Realization.

The ninth step is to reach our destination. Most of us think it is luck that decides our destiny. We don't discover the secret of twin Karma, the Karma we brought to Earth and the Karma we did after our birth. This twin Karma is what will unfold in life. While Attraction and Action will control what we do, we cannot control what has already been done in the past. This, we must understand, is true. Therefore, if we want to reach our destination, despite the circumstances, we can use Attraction and Action, and we will find a manifestation of our desires.

The tenth step of Attraction is to realize that our ultimate goal is Liberation and Unification. If we use Attraction to attract the material pleasures of this world, ultimately we will be sad because whatever we had would be left behind. Therefore, unless Attraction is led by Realization, our Action will go in the wrong direction. We must be clear about our intentions. We have to attain Liberation from all suffering on Earth and from the cycle of death and rebirth. One can use Attraction to reach that state of Divine Unification. But for this, we need Action, Action and Action.

The second last step, the eleventh step, is to let the magic of Attraction create a transformation. If we only take information and make it sparkle with Attraction, then there may be Action but we will not experience a transformation. Unfortunately, we have not realized the truth of what is our ultimate destination. When we have the right information and with the intellect, use our power of discrimination, we can experience a crystallization. This is only possible with the right Attraction and Action. If there is right guidance from an Enlightened Master and Divine grace is upon us, we will no longer crawl like a caterpillar. We will experience a transformation and fly like a butterfly. The ultimate goal of life is to let the transformation create a metamorphosis. This too is revealed in the book.

The twelfth and final step is to eliminate confusion. As long as our life is under the influence of our mind,

Introduction

Attraction will not inspire the right Action. Even if we put into Action our visualization, there will be no manifestation of Attraction because our own mind and its thoughts will create confusion. Therefore, there will be no concentration and there will not be enough passion that will take us to our ultimate destination. Hence, we must stop and overcome the myths and realize the truth. This is the final step for Attraction to work.

Wouldn't it be great if we sleep in our bed, put Attraction in our head and without doing anything, reach our destination before we are dead? Life doesn't work that way. We need to follow all the steps to reach Realization and Liberation. Most of us climb the first peak called achievement. We don't experience the second peak of fulfilment, which is built on the foundation of peace. Very few amongst us reach the ultimate peak of Enlightenment. But through Attraction and Action, we can reach our ultimate destination of Unification with the Supreme.

Are you ready to start the journey, to use the Law of Attraction with the secret ingredient, Action, to reach your destination? It's time to start. Don't just get into Action. First, attract the right thought and make sure you are not caught in toxic thoughts. Realize you can make any dream come true but pause and use your intellect to choose what you want to attract and what

Action Is the Secret to Attraction

you want to achieve in life. Once you start the process of Attraction and Action, you have chosen the direction and you lose control of the destination. Let there be this Realization. You have all the information. Now, it is time for implementation. If you follow it all, you will experience the moment of congratulation! It's time to get into Action.

WITHIN THE LAW OF ATTRACTION IS ACTION

There is a Law of Attraction
That can make any dream come true!
There is the power of visualization
That I use and so can you.
But 'Whatever we attract, it will manifest'.
Is this a myth or truth?
For this to know, look into Attraction
And you will get the clue!

Within Attraction, what do we see?
Embedded is the word 'Action'.
Of course, Attraction will work,
Sure, there will be manifestation.
Attraction has a lot of power,

Action Is the Secret to Attraction

For Attraction creates a passion.
Alas! This will just be a visualization,
If there is no Action.

For Attraction to work, then
We must discover the equation.
The equation is Attraction + Action,
This is the secret combination.
If we just depend on Attraction
Then there will be a powerful thought.
But thoughts without Action have no meaning,
In emptiness, we will be caught!

But those who discover the Law of Attraction
And they use the power to visualize,
They can manifest their dreams and goals,
Their passion they can actualize.
If one uses Attraction and Action,
Then their dream is sure to manifest.
If the combination is put into Action,
Then they will pass the test.

However, there is more to this,
It's not just the Law of Attraction.
Life is a journey to find meaning,
We must have direction.
If we get into Action

Within the Law of Attraction Is Action

And are not sure where we want to go,
Attraction will get us somewhere
But where, we won't even know.

The Law of Attraction is powerful
And we must use it at its best.
The Law of Action will always work,
These laws we don't need to test!
What is important is to find this out,
Who am I? Why am I here?
Then, Attraction and Action will work together
And our goals we will achieve for sure!

We human beings are the only ones
To be blessed with an intellect.
We have been given the power of discrimination
To choose, not do what is incorrect.
We must flip from NEP to PEP,
Negative to Positive, is the first step.
Then we can move from Mind to Consciousness
And be liberated from this worldly web!

Our ultimate goal is not success,
It is not just about achievement,
For this will give us pleasure.
But peace comes from fulfilment,
The ultimate peak that we must climb

Action Is the Secret to Attraction

Is where purpose has attainment.
This is the ultimate peak of joy,
This peak is called Enlightenment.

Whoever comes to this world suffers,
The body, mind and ego, have trauma.
Although we may succeed with Attraction,
We are all sure to be caught in this drama.
But those who realize the truth,
They celebrate knowing it is Karma.
They use Attraction and Action in the right way,
And ultimately attain Moksha.

The purpose of life is not just to live and die.
We must eliminate ignorance and get Realization.
It's no use, using the Law of Attraction
With just any information.
First, we must choose what is right,
We must use the power of discrimination.
Then we will experience the spark of light,
Illumination will lead to Realization.

Unless we go on a quest to find out,
What brought us to this Earth,
Unless we realize the truth that it was twin Karma
That decided our human birth,
Unless we go on a quest

Within the Law of Attraction Is Action

And attract the right direction,
Our Action will take us here and there,
And we won't reach our destination.

What is the ultimate goal of life?
From ignorance we must be free,
Not just to attract momentary pleasure
But from misery to be free!
And so, we must evolve beyond Attraction and Action
To Realization of the truth and transformation.
This will lead us to Liberation
And ultimately, Divine Unification.

So, let us be clear. Let there be no confusion.
Let us get to the conclusion.
The Law of Attraction is a powerful law,
But it cannot work without Action.
While Attraction and Action is a great combination,
It won't take us to our destination.
Unless there is Realization and transformation,
From misery there will be no Liberation.

It's time to discover the secret behind the secret,
Within Attraction to discover there is Action.
It's time to discover the secret equation,
Attraction and Action is the combination.
It's time to use visualization for transformation,

Action Is the Secret to Attraction

And not go in the wrong direction.
We must attain Realization and then Liberation.
Then Attraction will lead us to Unification.

STEP 1
DISCOVER THE
LAW OF ATTRACTION

There is Power in Attraction!
Visualization can lead to Manifestation.
But look deeper into the word 'Attraction',
Discover that within, is Action.

The Law of Attraction is a powerful phenomenon. It states that whatever you believe, you will achieve. Beliefs create thoughts. Thoughts create feelings. Feelings become Actions. Once an Action is performed, it will reach its logical conclusion as governed by the Law of Action. Therefore, Attraction is a law. Those who understand this law and discover the secret of how it works can opt for a destiny of their choice.

What are the Universal Laws of the world? These are the Laws created to govern how everything unfolds in the world. We are familiar with the Law of Gravity. It is a universal law and that is why, whatever we throw up in the sky, does not fly away. Similarly, the Sun rises and sets because the Earth rotates on its axis and revolves around the Sun. There is the Law of Action and Reaction; then there is birth and death. Everything happens as per the universal laws like the Law of Causation, the Law of Balance, the Law of Cycles and so on. So also there is the Law of Attraction.

How does the Law of Attraction actually work? It works on the principle *'As a man thinketh, so is he'*. Whatever we think, positive or negative, we will attract the corresponding result in our life. Attraction happens with visualization. First, there is a thought. It is like a seed we plant in our head. This thought germinates and becomes Attraction. Does it mean that every thought

Step 1: Discover the Law of Attraction

will reach its logical conclusion? No! When thought is powered by Attraction, and there is deep passion and obsession, this will lead us to Action. It is Action that makes the Law of Attraction work. Without Action, there can be no Attraction. That is why when you look deep within the word 'Attraction', you will find embedded within it the word 'Action'. Remove Action and there is no Attraction. But Attraction very often leads to Action, even though we may not want it. That is why we are warned, 'Beware of your thoughts', because once we are caught in a thought loop that thought will become an Action and there will be an Attraction of our visualization. Therefore, many global thinkers talk of Attraction as a law of manifestation. While it is true that Attraction is a Universal Law, it is equally true that there must be a combination of Attraction and Action.

> *'Whatever the mind of man can conceive and believe, it can achieve.'*
>
> —NAPOLEON HILL

Attraction is very powerful. If we continue to focus on a particular thought, and we keep repeating that thought in our head, that thought will not leave us until we are dead. Thoughts are very powerful, both positive and negative thoughts. If we intelligently choose a positive thought and apply the Law of Attraction, through conscious visualization of that thought, the logical conclusion is that the thought will become an Action and the Action will take us to our destination. However, if thoughts are not followed up with Action, then Attraction won't work. Attraction is very powerful when it is backed up by Action.

Ask and you shall receive. Seek and you will find. Knock and it will be opened (Mathew 7:7). What is the biblical meaning of what Jesus said? It only means that you can attract whatever you want, provided you follow it up with your deeds. It means Attraction will work provided there is Action.

> *'Envision the future you desire.*
> *Create the life of your dreams. See it, feel it, believe it.'*
>
> —JACK CANFIELD

Over the last few years, many authors and philosophers have launched the Law of Attraction as a secret to make our dreams come true. While they have done very well in sharing the secret, they have forgotten to emphasize the key that unlocks the door to using Attraction to manifest our dreams. No doubt, Attraction is a very powerful law but how does it work? There are many people around the world who are doing a lot to manifest their dreams. There are people who meditate on what they want to visualize. There are people who spend a lot of effort in scripting their manifestation. Is it true that just by repeating a thought or writing and rewriting a goal that the goal will manifest? Unless this is followed by the execution of Action, Attraction will remain unfulfilled. But just add Action to the recipe, and we are sure to make our dreams come true.

Therefore, while the first step is to discover the Law of Attraction, we must go through all the 12 steps to reach our final destination. Not only must we repeatedly work to bring anything into our life but we must also first untie the string that ties our wings. Then we can fly in the sky and make any dream come true. What according to authors and philosophers of the world is the Law of Attraction all about? Let us scan through their philosophy on Attraction and then let us use our power of discrimination to use Attraction to reach our destination.

Many people in the world have spoken about the Law of Attraction. Rhonda Byrne is the author of the world-famous book on Attraction, *The Secret*. In the book, she suggests that as per the Law of Attraction, positive thoughts and actions reap positive rewards and vice versa for negative ones. This is one of the 12 Universal Laws of the philosophy of Attraction. Therefore, the core of the philosophy is being positive because negative visualization will lead to negative manifestation. We have to be careful not to let autosuggestion create toxic results.

The Law of Attraction is a philosophy suggesting that positive thoughts bring positive results into a person's life, while negative thoughts bring negative outcomes. It is based on the belief that thoughts are a form of energy and that positive energy attracts success in all areas of life, including health, finances and relationships.

> The basic philosophy behind the Law of Attraction, as explained by Christy Whitman, is 'Energy precedes manifestation'. As such, positive thoughts may bring positive results into a person's life, while negative thoughts bring the opposite.[*]
>
> 'Whatever we direct our powerful focus upon within the invisible realm of our thoughts, beliefs and emotions eventually manifests into outer form,' claims Whitman. Thereby the Law of Attraction says the state of everything in our external world—our bodies, our relationships, the robustness of our careers and our finances—is a direct reflection of our internal state.

---

[*]Neumann, Kimberly Dawn, 'What Is The Law Of Attraction? A Complete Guide', *Forbes*, 20 February 2024, https://www.forbes.com/health/mind/what-is-law-of-attraction-loa/.

Step 1: Discover the Law of Attraction

The Law of Attraction is undoubtedly a powerful law of the universe. If one uses Attraction and creates a visualization, this power can definitely lead to manifestation. How can we use the power of Attraction and visualization? Let us move to step two to take the Law of Attraction forward and make it true so that whatever we attract in life, we can achieve if only we follow the steps from 1 to 12 in the Law of Attraction.

'Once you make a decision,
the universe conspires to make it happen.'

—RALPH WALDO EMERSON

ESSENCE OF STEP 1

DISCOVER THE LAW OF ATTRACTION

- The Law of Attraction is a Universal Law.
- It states that as we think, we become.
- While the Law of Attraction works, we must learn how to make it work.
- Just like the Law of Gravity, the Law of Karma or Action and the Law of Cycles, the Law of Attraction is one of the laws that govern this universe.
- If we look deeper into the word 'Attraction', we will find the word 'Action' embedded within.
- Attraction will work if we follow up our thoughts with Action.
- Many authors and philosophers have shared the Secret. But what is the secret behind the Secret?
- There are 12 steps to make Attraction really work.
- The first step is to discover the Law of Attraction.
- If there is the execution of all 12 steps of Attraction, there will surely be a manifestation and we will reach our destination.

STEP 2
UNDERSTAND THE POWER OF VISUALIZATION

*Visualization is the Power that can lead to Attraction.
When we light a fire to a thought and create passion,
Then this visualization becomes an obsession,
And Attraction will lead us to our destination.*

Action Is the Secret to Attraction

What makes the Law of Attraction work? What are the basic ingredients in Attraction that can make any dream come true? Attraction is a power. But how does this power work? It is through the power of visualization.

What is visualization? When we take a particular thought and create an image of that thought in our head, this image can either fade away into insignificance or it can become our life itself. When we capture a particular image of a dream, a goal, a wish or a desire and we add the power of visualization to it, this image drives us towards achieving it. Such is the power of visualization. Suppose you take a picture of your dream car and you paste this picture in your head, this has not yet become Attraction or visualization. But suppose you think of this dream car every day and now you visualize driving this car, you imagine taking your partner for a date and you picture yourself zooming down the highway in the car. Now you have taken a thought and converted that image into visualization. This can start the process of Attraction.

The Law of Attraction is not magic! It has some logic. And what is this logic? This is empowering the body and mind to feed on a powerful thought. In this moment, all our senses get tuned into trying to attract what we are visualizing. Visualization is not just with the eyes. Each

Step 2: Understand the Power of Visualization

of our senses is capable of adding to the visualization process and this is what really makes Attraction work.

> *'Logic will get you from A to B.*
> *Imagination will take you everywhere.'*
>
> —ALBERT EINSTEIN

Attraction becomes a law only when we discover the step-by-step method of putting Attraction into Action. If Attraction is just a weak wish, it will fizzle out. Haven't we heard the proverb *'If wishes were horses, beggars would ride'*? Attraction is not some silly process of making a wish come true. When one discovers the Law of Attraction, one gets into Action. Only then will Attraction work.

For the last four decades, I used the Law of Attraction by creating what I call an 'obsession statement'. Every year, I would visualize what I wanted to achieve. This dream would be born from my decade plan. I always had a plan for the next 10 years. Then, I created a pentad goal—what I would achieve in five years. I used to break this down into annual targets and create an obsession statement every year. I would visualize not just what I would achieve but also how I would do it. I would enumerate what all I needed to do. Then, I would paste this obsession statement everywhere—in my bedroom, on my desk and later, even on my laptop and mobile phone. I started to use the power of visualization to attract my dream. To me, after discovering the Law of Attraction, this was the most important step. If I had not used the power of visualization, then Attraction would have become a distraction. There would have been no focus, no priority, no power. What created power in Attraction? It was my visualization through my obsession statement.

> *'If you can dream it, you can do it.'*
> —TOM FITZGERALD

Just like we programme a device and thereafter the device acts, the human computer too needs to be programmed. The hardware of the human computer, the body, is driven by the human software, the mind. When there is visualization, then in the body–mind complex, the computer acts as per the program visualized, and the thought is realized. Therefore, if we want to make Attraction work, we must not only discover the power of Attraction but also understand the power of visualization and create an obsession. Then, we will be sailing on Attraction, and we will cross the shore to reach our destination.

If one discovers that there is a law called Attraction and one has some random thoughts on what they wish and

Step 2: Understand the Power of Visualization

hope for, then that is a weak proposition and does not have power. Attraction needs power. Unless the power of visualization is set on fire, Attraction won't work. Those who create a passion, execute the Law of Attraction. There must be a burning desire to achieve, and this is triggered by visualization. Not everybody understands how a powerful thought that is visualized, automatically becomes an Action. This is the next step but without visualization, no thought will lead to manifestation.

'You become what you think about all day long.'
—RALPH WALDO EMERSON

If Attraction was a magical law, the world would not face so much disappointment and heartbreak. Everybody would achieve their dreams and goals. Success would be easy, and it would not be a challenge to marry the dream of our lives. But does all this happen easily? No! Only those of us who use the power of visualization create a passion, an obsession, that ultimately leads us to Action are the ones who make success possible. Dreams do come true but there must be a follow through. Visualization is the key. When our visualization has passion, it will create a spark of Action.

The biggest challenge in visualization is that it does not differentiate between good and bad, positive and negative.

Action Is the Secret to Attraction

Even if you have a toxic thought and keep visualizing it, the toxic thought will materialize because of the Law of Attraction. Therefore, we must be very careful with what we visualize and what we think. Just discovering the Law of Attraction is not enough. Our challenge is to intelligently choose our thoughts and not get caught in the toxic mind that can make us blind.

Naomi believed in the Law of Attraction. She believed that this was the secret of life, that whatever she attracted would manifest. She kept on attracting the man of her dreams. She even spent time being intimate with him, spending weekends for several months hoping that he would become her life partner. She had no doubt! She had visualized it and attracted it. It seemed that the secret truly worked. However, Naomi lived in fear—what if she lost the love of her life? These thoughts became strong but her insecurity did not come in the way of her passion for her beloved. However, one day, he walked out of her life! She wondered why this happened.

The problem with this law is that even if you think of something that you don't want, it is said that you will attract it. The law doesn't distinguish between good and bad. It only attracts whatever you think. If you are thinking about success, you will attract success but if you are thinking of failure, you are sure to fail. The law simply gives you back whatever you are 'thinking' about.

Step 2: Understand the Power of Visualization

People have different things to say about the Law of Attraction. Some say it is a very natural law and shows results if we follow it. If only we focus on what we want with all our attention, we will attract that into our life. If you focus, for instance, that you don't want to be fat, the law doesn't recognize 'don't' and you may become fat because the law will attract what you focus on. Instead, you must focus on being thin. So, you mustn't focus on something that you don't want. There was somebody, for instance, who focused on 'I don't want to be late'. What do you think would have happened?

The Law of Attraction is the Law of Visualization. If only you had a mind that could imagine something, you could visualize it and soon, what you visualized would manifest in your life. Such is the law! Thus, the law is a Law of Imagination. Whatever you imagine in your life, you will attract just because you think, you visualize and you imagine it. Therefore, this law could be called the Law of Expectation, of Visualization or of Imagination, and not just Attraction.

Suppose you want to be a billionaire, then just think of being a billionaire. As W. Clement Stone said, *'Whatever the mind of man can conceive and believe, it can achieve.'* The Law of Attraction states that if you think about being a billionaire consistently and you send out this message into the universe, you will ultimately become a billionaire. Such is the Law of Attraction! It all depends on our thoughts. All we must do is focus on wealth. Imagine that you already have wealth. Imagine already receiving that wealth in your bank! Think wealth, seek wealth, attract wealth, think billionaire and you will become a billionaire. There are other people who share amazing love stories and how they attracted the most beautiful relationships in their lives.

Once we have the right visualization, we are on our way. The process of thoughts, feelings and actions will automatically lead visualization to manifestation. The Law of Attraction is set in motion but we need to follow the logical steps to get to where we want to go. Are you ready for the next step?

> *'A man can only rise, conquer, and achieve*
> *by lifting up his thoughts.'*
>
> —JAMES ALLEN

ESSENCE OF STEP 2

UNDERSTAND THE POWER OF VISUALIZATION

- To make the Law of Attraction work, we must use the power of visualization.
- Attraction is all about taking a thought and making it an obsession.
- When there is a visualization of our dream, we create a passion.
- When visualization lights a fire through repeated imagination, then that thought becomes unstoppable.
- The challenge is that visualization doesn't consider what is good or bad, positive or negative.
- When Attraction uses visualization, we create a passion that will push us in that direction.
- If we effectively use visualization and follow all the steps, we can make our dreams come true!

STEP 3
USE THE THOUGHT-CHAIN FOR MANIFESTATION

Thoughts are the starting point
Of making dreams come true,
What you think, feel and act will manifest, this is true!
So take charge of your destiny
Through your thought-chain,
Visualize what you want and repeat it again and again!

How can one use the Law of Attraction to make things happen? If one has discovered the Law, one realizes that it is not some magic. It has a clear logic. One has to follow a step-by-step method to manifest desires. It is not enough to understand the Law of Attraction and the power of visualization. One must use the thought-chain for manifestation. This is the third step in the 12-step method of converting Attraction to Action.

To make any delicious meal, we need all the ingredients and a good recipe to cook it. So it is with Attraction. No doubt, good use of the Universal Law can lead to manifestation. There are people who script or write their dreams every day. They believe that just by programming their mind and using the power of autosuggestion, Attraction will lead to manifestation. But is this true? One needs to understand the thought-chain and the process that will take Attraction to its logical conclusion.

> *'There is nothing either good or bad,
> but our thinking makes it so.'*
>
> —SHAKESPEARE

It all starts with a thought. Therefore, those who discover the Law of Attraction are very cautious of what they think. They know that if they are caught in a thought, that

Step 3: Use the Thought-Chain for Manifestation

thought will be brought into their lives. Why? Because thoughts are the starting point. Thoughts become feelings and these feelings become Action. It is like a chain, one leading to the next. It is like a train. The speed of the engine is the speed of the train. As is the thought, so will be the Action and the destination. The thought will give direction. One who understands the thought-chain can use the power of Attraction and visualization for manifestation.

> *'Think the thought until you believe it,
> and once you believe it, it is.'*
>
> —ABRAHAM HICKS

Therefore, we must be very clear that the key to Attraction is thought. Suppose you think, 'I want to be thin'. Then the word 'thin' becomes the thought. You will programme all your actions to becoming thin. But instead, if the thought is 'I don't want to be fat', the mind may pick the word 'fat' and you may attract and gain weight. Therefore, we must not visualize what we don't want, rather what we want. This is key in visualization and thought creation.

Once the right thought is planted like a seed, we need the deed, which is the next step. There are 12 steps that will lead us to the conclusion and we must understand why each step is important. Some people think that thought is everything. Is it true? If you just think that you will be a millionaire, will you be one? Of course not! Then, everybody in this world will achieve all their dreams. Those who learn how the thought-chain works, understand the importance of being consistent in thought. A repeated thought creates repeated feelings and Actions. It is a repeated Action that creates habits and our character that leads to our destiny. Therefore, Thoughts create Feelings. Feelings create Actions. Actions create Habits. Habits create Character and Character creates Destiny. This is the thought-chain. Unless we understand the thought-chain, manifestation will remain a dream.

'Nurture your mind with great thoughts, for you will never go any higher than you think.'

—BENJAMIN DISRAELI

One must use the power of thought and not be caught by the mind that wanders from thought to thought. Attraction has power, provided one's visualization of a particular thought becomes a passion, an obsession and takes them to their destiny.

Weak thoughts cannot cause Attraction. Weak feelings will not create discrete Action and will not take us to our destination. Therefore, we must take charge

Step 3: Use the Thought-Chain for Manifestation

of our thoughts. How can we choose our thoughts? First, we must realize the truth about the mind. Have you ever seen the mind? Nobody has! Still, the mind seems to exist. It seems to be a thought factory that is constantly producing thoughts. Thoughts come from different parts of our body, from every sense perception. Can we control thought? Yes, we can. Just like we can control what any factory produces by controlling the raw material we supply, so we can control our thought factory, the mind, by providing the right raw material. The raw material is emotions. If we provide positive emotions, we can produce positive thoughts. However, if we provide negative emotions, the mind will produce negative thoughts. Therefore, choosing what emotion we supply to the thought factory, the mind, is key to what will be the manifestation through Attraction.

*'Imagination is everything,
it is the preview of life's coming attractions.'*

—UNKNOWN

Manifestation depends on visualization. It depends on the thought we visualize, positive or negative. Whatever is the contemplation, so will be the Action. But without Action, will there be any Attraction? Many people who do not understand the thought-chain, do not realize that a thought by itself cannot lead to manifestation.

Action Is the Secret to Attraction

The thought-chain must be completed. Unless there is Action, Attraction can't be manifested. So is thought not important? Beware. Thought is very, very important. Because it is thought that will lead to Action. Without thought, there will be no Action and what you do directly depends on what you think. So don't hesitate in what you think. Don't blink, for then you cannot manifest what you attract. It is not possible to think something and do something else. The thought-chain will not permit it. Therefore, understanding Attraction and the thought-chain and then getting into Action are logical steps that we must follow to reach our destination.

If we don't understand the thought-chain, we will wonder why despite visualization of thought, we have not achieved anything. We don't realize that nothing will happen without Action. If thought is followed by Action, nothing can stop the conclusion. Sometimes, it is the other way round. We try to work very hard but nothing seems to happen. We don't realize that it is our thoughts that are taking us away from manifestation. We don't realize that there is no powerful visualization of thought, and therefore, no Attraction of our dreams.

Do you want to use the Law of Attraction to make your dream come true? It's time to discover how Attraction works, how important visualization is and how manifestation depends on your thoughts. You can choose

Step 3: Use the Thought-Chain for Manifestation

your thoughts by choosing your emotions and choosing your attitude. If you choose to behave, react and respond in a particular way, you will manifest that. Therefore, carefully control your thought-chain. Take charge of your mind and the raw material you fill in it. Watch your feelings and your moods, for they will germinate into Action. Do an audit of your habits and reflect on the character your thoughts have created. If they are not in line with what you want to achieve, it's time to get to the root and change your thought. Otherwise, you will continue to get the same fruit from the same shoot. Manifestation is not magic. It is a result of visualization of Attraction, which is automatically put into Action by the thought-chain. However, if we do not follow the thought-chain with Action, there can be no Attraction, no manifestation. Let's use the thought-chain to make our dreams come true.

> *'What you think, you become. What you feel, you attract. What you imagine, you create.'*
>
> —THE BUDDHA

ESSENCE OF STEP 3

USE THE THOUGHT-CHAIN FOR MANIFESTATION

- Manifestation depends on the visualization of thought.
- Visualization cannot lead to Attraction without Action.
- Everything depends on thoughts. They are the starting point.
- We must use the thought-chain again and again.
- Thoughts lead to Feelings. Feelings lead to Actions.
- Actions lead to Habits. Habits build our Character.
- Our Character leads us to our Destiny.
- If we control our thought, we can take charge of our destiny, provided we use the thought-chain effectively.
- Be careful of your thoughts. What you think, you will become, and you will achieve.
- Ultimately, we control our thoughts through the raw material we feed our thought factory.

STEP 4
GET INTO ACTION, ACTION, ACTION

Can you achieve your dream with just Attraction?
Attraction is the start. The end is Action.
If there is only Attraction, there is only thought.
Then in unfulfilled dreams, our life will be caught.

Action Is the Secret to Attraction

Do you want the Law of Attraction to work in your life? Do you want to experience manifestation that comes from visualization? The key is step four—Get into Action, Action, Action.

There can be no Attraction without Action. The word 'Attraction' itself reveals this. From 'Attraction', remove 'Action'. What is left? Nothing! 'ATTR'—A Thought That Roams. A roaming thought can get nowhere. You may attract something for all your life. But without Action, there can be no Attraction. Does it mean that Attraction is of no use? Of course not! Attraction is the root. Action is the shoot that will deliver the fruit. Can there be fruit without the root and the shoot? If we want that fruit, that manifestation, then choose the root carefully. The root is thought. Thought is what will create the Action. But unless we get into Action, we cannot convert the root into fruit.

'The universe doesn't give you what you ask for with your thoughts—it gives you what you demand with your actions.'

—STEVE MARABOLI

The Law of Action is a Universal Law. It is known as the Law of Karma. It is the Law of Action and Reaction, a Law of Cause and Effect. Some people call it the Law of Boomerang—what goes around comes around. This

Step 4: Get into Action, Action, Action

law is based on the principle, *'As you sow, so shall you reap'*. Nobody can escape from the Law of Karma. The Law is so powerful that not only does life unfold as per Karma but all unsettled Karma is also carried forward into a new birth, a rebirth on Earth. Who decided our birth? Did we decide our parents, our gender or our nationality when we came to Earth? We didn't do it. It was Karma that decided that. When we understand the Law of Karma, we understand how the Law of Attraction works. The Law of Attraction is very powerful but within this Law lies the Law of Action. The Law of Attraction will be incomplete without the Law of Action.

'The ancestor of every action is a thought.'
—RALPH WALDO EMERSON

Suppose I have a bad thought. Will I pay for this sin? A bad thought is not a bad Karma. If I am able to overcome the bad thought, there is no sin. We have no direct control over all our thoughts. We can influence our thoughts by the emotions we feed the mind with. But ultimately, we do not control thought. But we do control Action. We can intercept thought, discriminate, choose and stop Action from happening. However, if we let the thought become passion, even an obsession, then it is impossible to stop Action. Therefore, some people believe that Attraction is everything. While this is true,

Action Is the Secret to Attraction

without Action, there will be no conclusion. We may have a very noble thought. We may have some amazing ideals and a good philosophy. But what are thoughts without deeds? If one has a great idea but there is no implementation, then that information remains just an idea, a thought. There will be no manifestation. Therefore, Karma is Action. It is a Law of Action and Reaction. Whatever is our Action, so will be the reaction.

People believe in luck. They don't realize that there is nothing like luck. Whatever is unfolding in our life is not our luck but rather what we pluck. Once we have planted the seed, the seed will bear fruit. So our deeds that are already done are like seeds. They become the cause. The effect has to manifest. We cannot change the effect of the cause already performed by any magic. If we have planted mangoes, we cannot desire that they become apples. If we manifest apples and this leads us to planting apple trees, then in the future, we will reap apples. But nothing can stop mangoes growing on the tree if the mango seed is planted. So, Action becomes the most important aspect of Attraction. Those who don't realize this will be using visualization all their lives but there will be no manifestation if there is no Action.

The Law of Attraction, therefore, has 12 steps that will take us to our destination. Those who don't discover the

Step 4: Get into Action, Action, Action

Law, don't use the power of thought. Those who discover the Law use visualization to light a fire on their ideas. But unless we understand the thought-chain, which is step three, we will not reach the crucial step four of Action.

There are eight more steps that are key to reach our destination. If we use all these 12 steps, we can make any dream come true. But even the execution of these 12 steps can't happen by Attraction. It needs Action. Those who are fortunate enough to get their hands on the 12 steps that can create a transformation of visualization into manifestation, realize that nothing is possible without Action.

Action is a Law, a Universal Law. Nobody in this world can escape from it. While Attraction is a very powerful phenomenon and therefore considered to be the Law of Attraction, the real Law that is unstoppable is the Law of Action. No doubt it is a Law that Attraction creates visualization but some people argue that how can Attraction be a law if everything that we attract and manifest does not bear fruit? The power of Attraction is phenomenal. But within Attraction lies Action. This is a secret that fills our history and therefore, Attraction remains a mystery. Those who understand Attraction, get into Action. Even visualization or manifestation needs Action. Just roaming random thoughts can be vicious and there will be no crystallization of our dreams and goals.

Action Is the Secret to Attraction

But once the Law of Action is plugged into Attraction, it is impossible for anything to stop the unfolding of this equation.

The Law of Action is universally accepted. Today, people from all countries, cultures and religions accept Karma. More and more people are trying to do good Karma because they know that everything that is unfolding in life is unfolding as per Karma. A few people understand that Karma doesn't end at death. When the body dies, there is always unsettled Karma that leads to a rebirth. Some people understand and accept this, while others don't! It has no real relevance to Attraction. It is only a further understanding of the Law of Action and how it works.

The ultimate goal of Attraction is to be happy. But it is Action or Karma that teaches us the way to eternal bliss. Doing good Karma will give happiness but transcending Karma will liberate us from all misery and sorrow. If we use the power of thought, visualization, to reach that state of Liberation, then we have effectively used information for a transformation. When we let Attraction be a random thing, we may achieve success, money, name and fame but this achievement leads to momentary happiness. When we go into the depth of Karma, then we are blessed to understand *Moksha, Nirvana* and Salvation. All these are different words but they mean the same

Step 4: Get into Action, Action, Action

thing—Liberation from Karma. If we make Attraction a matter of purification and illumination, then we can reach the ultimate destination of Unification with the Divine. Not many people are blessed to take Action on this visualization.

Most people are enamoured by the Attraction of pleasure. They do not evolve to a state of peace—the basic foundation of happiness. A few go further to attract the purpose of our existence. They use Attraction for Realization of the Truth. Their Action leads to Self-realization and even God-realization. But can this just happen with Attraction?

> 'Man, alone, has the power to transform his thoughts into physical reality; man, alone, can dream and make his dreams come true.'
>
> —NAPOLEON HILL

Unless we get into Action and go on a quest, we will never realize the truth. We have to dig deep and go to the root. We have to question, what are we attracting? We have to escape from being caught in thought. We have to activate our intellect to discriminate. Otherwise, the circle of Attraction will become a distraction from the real purpose of our existence. It's time to stop and take stock of what we are trying to attract in our life.

Action Is the Secret to Attraction

It's time for discrimination of our visualization. It's time to get into Action, to take the help of an enlightened one so that we take the right direction to reach the ultimate destination.

It is so important to understand the Law of Action, because without the Law of Action, Attraction will cease to be a Law. It will just be a powerful phenomenon. But when the Law of Attraction is built upon the Law of Action, nothing can stop this combination of Attraction + Action to reach its ultimate destination. Yes, we can make any dream come true. We can manifest any thought, provided we use the steps required. The key steps are Attraction and Action. Attraction will lead to visualization but it is Action that will cause the ultimate manifestation. It is time to move to the fifth step to discover the secret equation that will take us to our destination.

> *'Everything you want is out there waiting for you to ask.*
> *Everything you want also wants you.*
> *But you have to take action to get it.'*
>
> —JACK CANFIELD

Karma is a well-known concept in Eastern civilizations and while by itself, it means Action, it has become popular around the world to denote the Law of Action. Therefore,

Step 4: Get into Action, Action, Action

when somebody says 'Karma', they are referring to the Law of Action.

Something happens in life—an accident, unexpected good luck, a tragedy or an unexpected reward—people echo 'Karma'. What does it mean? It means that the circumstances that are unfolding are not pure luck or serendipity. They are the result of past Actions that appear as reactions in our life. Those who understand the Law of Karma know beyond doubt that nothing in this world happens to us just by chance. It is the result of our deeds. It is just like the seeds that cause the flowers and fruits to grow in our garden. There would be no roses and no apples if we had not planted the respective seeds.

While the whole world is aware, beyond doubt, of this Universal Law that is based on the principle *'As you sow, so shall you reap'*, they have not discovered the true meaning of the Law of Karma. The law states, *'What you give, is what you get.'* Isn't it true that what you do comes back to you? Don't we see kindness being returned by kindness in our life? Don't we notice that just like a boomerang, what goes around comes around?

Why, then, do some people question the Law of Karma? It is because they have not discovered the principle behind the law. They see bad things happen to seemingly good people and they ask, 'Why do bad things happen to good people?' They don't realize that bad things can't happen to good people, just like apples can't grow on mango trees. It's time to discover the Law of Karma!

Mrs and Mr Jones lived a pious life. Not only did they believe in God and spend their time in prayer but they also used to go and serve people who were suffering every week, with different social service groups. They had two lovely children—Tom and Susan—who were in their teens. They were a very happy family.

One day, their son, while swimming with his friends in a nearby lake, drowned. They were devastated. They folded their hands and asked God, 'Why? What wrong have we done that you took our boy away from us? He was a young, innocent boy!' They didn't find any answers to their questions and their faith was shattered. They even stopped going to serve the poor, as they could not decide whether God was cruel or so helpless that he could not save their only son.

Mrs and Mr Jones lost their zest for life. Just as they were mourning the loss of their son, they received the sad news that their daughter had died in a car accident! They were shocked beyond words. They couldn't believe it! It seemed that their entire world had come to an end. They shut themselves in their home for several months till one day, a dear friend brought a monk to their place. With eyes that seemed to have lost all their tears, they asked the monk, 'What kind of world is this where both our children have been taken away from us? What wrong have

Step 4: Get into Action, Action, Action

we done?' The Spiritual Master replied, 'Karma is a Law that we cannot escape from. It doesn't let us escape even after death. It records our past deeds and redeems both our sins and our acts of service, compassion and love.'

'Nothing happens by chance,' the Master explained. 'God is neither cruel nor helpless. We have to surrender to Karma and accept the Divine Will that unfolds. Whatever happens in this world, is not luck, fate or serendipity. It is the deeds that we have already done that unfold in our life.' He tried to explain to them that we must accept the Law of Karma because we don't have a choice. If there is something we have done, Karma will ensure it is settled.

This should give us a basic introduction about Karma, the Law of Action and how it influences Attraction. Having understood both the Law of Attraction and the Law of Action, the next step will reveal a secret equation.

> 'Karma is a Universal Law,
> What you sow is what you shall reap.
> Your good deeds will bear fruit,
> And for your sins, you will weep.'
>
> —AiR

ESSENCE OF STEP 4

GET INTO ACTION, ACTION, ACTION

- If you want Attraction to work, you need Action.
- Without Action, there can be no Attraction.
- Action is a law known as Karma. It is a Law of Cause and Effect, a Law of Action and Reaction.
- This Universal Law is based on the principle *'As you sow, so shall you reap'*.
- Nobody can escape from the Law of Action.
- Action is triggered by thought. Therefore, Attraction is the root. Action is the shoot that will determine the fruit.
- When the Law of Action is plugged into the Law of Attraction, it becomes unstoppable! Then one will achieve manifestation.
- If you remove 'Action' from 'Attraction', what is left is just 'ATTR'—A Thought That Roams.

STEP 5
ACTIVATE THE SECRET EQUATION: ATTRACTION + ACTION

Do you want to reach your destination?
It's time to discover the secret equation.
If you activate Attraction + Action,
You will succeed in your manifestation.

Action Is the Secret to Attraction

The secret is revealed. The Law of Attraction is a phenomenal law. But within the Law of Attraction is embedded the Law of Action. If one wants the Law of Attraction to work, one has to activate both. Then, one can use the power of visualization for the manifestation of their dreams and goals.

We have reached the fifth step of making Attraction work. To reflect, most of the world is unaware that the Law of Attraction exists. Thus, people do not use the power of thought to make things happen. In fact, inadvertently, they are caught in toxic thoughts, and this is what they attract, although they don't want it. Attraction is a choice. We can choose to attract what we like, although thinking is not a choice all the time. Negative thoughts may bombard us but those who discover the Law of Attraction realize that they can choose positive over negative. But this is the next step.

Just discovering the law is not enough. Just visualizing success won't make dreams come true. No doubt visualization has power, for the more we think and visualize, the more that thought not only gets planted in our head but it replays again and again, whether we are awake or whether we are asleep. The mind is a thought factory. Its job is to constantly produce thoughts. It may produce a new thought or a repeated thought. It may produce toxic thoughts or nourishing thoughts. If we

Step 5: Activate the Secret Equation: Attraction + Action

don't feed the thought factory with positive raw material, by default, it may produce more negative than positive thoughts. Therefore, Attraction works with visualization.

> *'Thoughts become things. If you see it in your mind, you will hold it in your hand.'*
>
> —BOB PROCTOR

Not many people can understand the thought-chain. Many authors and philosophers say, 'Think Positive!' but the challenge is how to think positive. Libraries and bookshops are filled with books on positive attitude. But is it easy to react, to respond, to behave with a positive attitude? Our attitude will depend on the emotions by which we live. If we don't choose positive emotions, we cannot have a positive attitude. Negative thoughts will flood our mind. Therefore, understanding all this is a prerequisite for getting into Action.

One who has mastered the Law of Attraction can make any dream come true. However, the secret is to combine Attraction and Action. It is this combination that will take us to our destination. We must activate this secret equation.

The secret equation is Attraction + Action. If we use the power of Attraction and follow it up with Action, nobody can stop us from achieving our dreams and goals.

Action Is the Secret to Attraction

If there are people who are struggling in life, despite using this secret equation of Attraction + Action, they need to go through all the 12 steps listed in this book to audit where they are stuck. Most likely, Attraction + Action will take us to our destination. But do we have a complete command over what we are attracting, thinking and visualizing? Is our Action on the same frequency as our Attraction? Unless both Action and Attraction work in tandem, hand in hand, there will be no activation of this secret equation.

Suppose I dream of becoming a champion in sports. The dream is just the beginning. I have to work at it. It may need physical practice just as it will require developing the skills. I will have to find an expert coach and then get into Action. If I visualize my dream with passion and there is a reflection of how I am progressing in the direction of my dream, there are good chances I will reach my goal. Of course, it needs passion. We must invest time and energy. We have to work hard and smart. Everybody cannot be successful. But those who use the secret equation of Attraction + Action have the advantage over anybody else.

It is strange that although this recipe is available to the world, only a few people use the Law of Attraction to succeed. There are others who work hard but their Action lacks the passion that comes from Attraction. Blessed are

Step 5: Activate the Secret Equation: Attraction + Action

those who discover the secret equation of Attraction + Action. When they activate this combination, they achieve success.

Where are you on the journey of Attraction and Action? It's time to do an audit before moving forward. Are you ahead in the combination, the secret equation, or do you need to improve on either Attraction or Action? If both are at their best, the chances are you are a success in what you want and what you do. The rest of the steps will take you beyond achievement and success. They will go beyond Attraction and Action to make you reach your ultimate destination in life. But all this is based on discrimination, which is the next step. Thereafter, the Law of Attraction and Action will evolve to a higher peak still unknown to many. Whether we are seeking the first peak of achievement or the second peak of fulfilment, it is the secret equation of Attraction + Action that will take us there. Even the third and ultimate peak of happiness in life needs activation of the secret equation of Attraction + Action. If we want Self-realization, Liberation or Salvation that will lead to God-realization, this ultimate peak needs the secret equation of Attraction + Action.

The world thinks that the Law of Attraction is a secret. Many people think of it as some magical phenomenon of visualization to reach our dream destination. The truth is that there is no magic. It is simple logic. Thoughts are seeds that we plant. Then we need deeds. Together, they determine our destiny. The secret behind the secret of Attraction is the secret equation—Attraction + Action. If one activates this, one will reach their destination. The secret will be a secret no more!

*'Each day of my life I am sowing seeds
that one day I will harvest.'*

—THE BUDDHA

ESSENCE OF STEP 5

ACTIVATE THE SECRET EQUATION: ATTRACTION + ACTION

- The Law of Attraction is very powerful. But does all Attraction end in manifestation?

- Unless one uses the Law of Action, Attraction will remain a dream.

- There is a secret equation that works. It is Attraction + Action.

- If we activate the secret equation, can we reach our destination?

- People think Attraction is the secret. But there is a secret behind that secret.

- There is no magic! It is all simple logic. A step-by-step way: visualization, Attraction, Action, manifestation.

STEP 6
CHOOSE POSITIVE OVER NEGATIVE THROUGH DISCRIMINATION

We have a choice to choose NEP or PEP,
This, in fact, is the very first step!
If the power of discrimination we don't use,
Our dreams and goals, we are sure to lose!

Action Is the Secret to Attraction

If we discover the secret equation—Attraction + Action, will we reach our desired destination? No! We may desire something but our mind may plant a negative toxic thought in our head and then we are dead! This negative thought will become a seed. There will be visualization and manifestation of this negative thought, which is not our desired dream. Because Attraction is so powerful, when the mind repeats this toxic thought, then this toxic thought germinates. The roots create toxic shoots and fruits and before we realize it, our dream is overpowered by the toxic thought and we reach the wrong destination.

Imagine planting some beautiful plants in your garden. You plant them and water them and you are looking forward to having a beautiful garden. But what happens if you see weeds growing all over? You did not plant these wild weeds. Where did they come from? There is no doubt that these weeds did not come out by magic. We understand the logic that these weeds are because of seeds that were dropped by birds or by the wind or by some other means. But they did not appear by magic. What must we learn from this analogy? We have to be careful to uproot the weeds from our thought garden. We need to use the power of discrimination. Otherwise, despite discovering the secret equation of Attraction + Action, we will not reach our destination.

Step 6: Choose Positive Over Negative through Discrimination

> *'Change your thoughts and you change your world.'*
> —NORMAN VINCENT PEALE

What are we seeking? We must have complete clarity. The Law of Attraction tells us to focus on what we want. Don't focus on what you don't want because if you do, that focus will manifest in your life. Therefore, those who discover the Law of Attraction understand the power of visualization. They realize that thought is the key and if one is caught in a wrong thought, then one will attract a destiny one did not seek. Therefore, the sixth step in making Attraction work is discrimination.

We, human beings, have been given an intellect that can discriminate black from white, wrong from right. We must discriminate positive from negative and must make a conscious choice of the dreams that we seek. We must completely eliminate the negative thoughts that we don't want. If we do not use discrimination, then just like our garden developed weeds, our mind will develop toxic seeds that will bear toxic fruit.

Those who read about Attraction learn that the power of visualization works without discrimination. What does this mean? It means once you visualize a thought, then there is no possibility of stopping that thought from germinating and producing shoots and fruits. Therefore, it is important to stop the thought at the seed stage before it is planted. We have to uproot all toxic thoughts and not let any toxic thoughts control our life. Only then will our positive thoughts help us achieve our dreams and goals.

For this, we must sharpen the tool called intellect. The intellect shines in Consciousness. If we do not kill the mind, it will disable the power of the intellect and therefore, our ability to discriminate will be lost. Then negative thoughts will overtake positive thoughts and soon, the garden in our head will be filled with weeds of negativity. Therefore, in the journey of Attraction and Action, the sixth step of discrimination is key. Otherwise, we will experience a wrong implementation of Attraction. Unwanted negative thoughts that enter our head will create negative visualization and lead to negative manifestation. Then we will wonder why the Law of Attraction has failed.

The Law of Attraction never fails. We fail in discrimination. We fail because we permit negative thoughts to overtake positive thoughts. Sometimes, we don't even realize that inadvertently, when we don't choose positive thoughts, we create a vacuum and permit the monkey mind to fill our head with toxic thoughts. Therefore, this calls for another warning. There is no scope for inaction in discrimination. We must consciously be aware of what thoughts we choose, just as we must consciously eliminate toxic thoughts.

Step 6: Choose Positive Over Negative through Discrimination

Somebody asked, 'What can I do when a toxic thought enters my head?' The answer is simple: 'Be in consciousness. Activate the intellect. Use the power of discrimination. When that toxic thought tries to enter— STOP IT, CROP IT, CHOP IT AND DROP IT! Flush it out of your system completely. Don't let such a thought enter your head, for once it does, thoughts become feelings that become Action. This will result in Attraction of a wrong thought.' Therefore, beware of inaction and live with discrimination. Then, the Laws of Attraction and Action will help you to reach your destination.

We, human beings, have a choice. We can choose PEP or NEP. PEP is Positive Energy that has Power. NEP is Negative Energy that has Poison. If we let NEP become the raw material of our mind, the weeds of negative thinking destroy our mind. What are some of these negative emotions? Fear, worry, stress, anxiety, regret, shame, guilt, anger, hate, revenge, jealousy and pessimism. The thought of these poisonous toxic emotions is enough to steal our enthusiasm. Through the power of discrimination, we must eliminate all NEP from our life. Every time NEP tries to enter, we must replace the negative emotion with a positive emotion. This is a choice. What raw material we choose to feed the mind, our thought factory is in our hands. But once we feed negative raw material, we are doomed. This will lead to negative thoughts and reactions. How, then, can we expect a positive visualization to take us to our destination?

Through discrimination, we must learn to flip over from NEP to PEP. The positive emotions of PEP will give us energy and inspiration. What are some of the PEP emotions? They are faith, hope, trust, enthusiasm, courage, confidence, compassion, forgiveness, love and optimism. When we choose these emotions, they result in us living in peace and joy, and the thoughts that are planted in our head will germinate into the positive dreams and goals that we seek. But we must use our willpower to make a choice. We must use the gift of discrimination, which is a unique gift to humanity. If we lose the opportunity to discriminate, then we lose control of our fate. Our destiny is in our hands. But not without discrimination. It is discriminating and choosing PEP over NEP that will give us the power to climb our tower of success. If we don't choose, we are sure to lose—and this is a choice!

> *'I attract to my life whatever I give my attention, energy and focus to, whether positive or negative.'*
>
> —MICHAEL LOSIER

ESSENCE OF STEP 6

CHOOSE POSITIVE OVER NEGATIVE THROUGH DISCRIMINATION

- If we want the Law of Attraction to work, we must use our power of discrimination.
- We have to choose positive over negative thoughts.
- If we don't use this unique gift of discrimination, we will lose the power of Attraction.
- Whatever thoughts we attract, they will manifest. So, we must uproot all negative thoughts.
- While we cannot always control thought, we can control the raw material that we feed our mind and which influences our thoughts and attitude.
- We must eliminate NEP, Negative Energy Poison, emotions like fear, worry, stress and anxiety.
- We must choose PEP, Positive Energy Power, emotions like faith, enthusiasm, courage, confidence and optimism.
- Finally, if there is no discrimination, we will not reach our desired destination.

STEP 7
BE IN CONSCIOUSNESS
FOR PURIFICATION

What is the journey of Attraction + Action?
It is to achieve our dream, our destination.
But unless we live in Consciousness with Purification,
We will be going in the wrong direction!

The seventh step to make the Law of Attraction work is purification. If we have to discriminate negative from positive and choose positive thoughts, then this process of discrimination can be completed if we can transcend the mind, be in Consciousness and attain that state of purification in thought and deed. At this stage, it is also imperative that we start moving towards our ultimate destination—Enlightenment, using the Laws of Attraction and Action to manifest our spiritual destiny. Of course, ultimately it's a choice. We can continue to apply the Laws of Attraction and Action to manifest our worldly desires. But to what end? The sooner we realize the futility of craving for and collecting wealth, fortune, the futility of running the race to become an ace, the better it is. We must draw a line and evolve in life. We must evolve from a life of achievement to fulfilment and ultimately to Enlightenment, just as we must evolve from the mind state to Consciousness.

So what is it to be in Consciousness? While we understand that thought is very powerful, not many of us understand that the mind is our enemy. The mind is a rascal. Has anybody seen the mind? Although it appears to exist but the truth is that the mind just doesn't. It is only a bundle of thoughts. Therefore, however much we try to find the mind, 'Where is the mind? We cannot find.' When several toxic thoughts gather, the mind appears. But in

Step 7: Be in Consciousness for Purification

reality, the mind is illusory. It doesn't exist. What we must learn is that Attraction is to do with thought and not to do with the mind, for the mind makes us blind. It tries to hide the truth of life because if we realize the truth then the mind will cease to exist. Of course, the mind appears to exist but have you ever seen the mind? You can touch your nose, pull your ears, you can see an X-ray or an MRI of the heart or the brain but have you ever seen the mind? What is its shape? Where does it exist? Nobody has seen the mind. Nobody can see the mind because the mind doesn't exist. It only appears when it bundles up thoughts and kills us.

We have all heard of the dreaded weapon AK-47. But have we heard of the weapon MK-50? The MK-50 is the Mind-Killer 50. The mind that is created out of ignorance appears and shoots at us a thought practically every second. This can become 50,000 thoughts a day as it attacks us with 50 thoughts every minute. As long as we are under the influence of the illusory mind, we will attract what the mind decides and desires. Unfortunately, the mind is by default a negative instrument and unless we make an effort to choose positive thoughts, positive emotions and a positive attitude, the mind will drill us and kill us with toxic negative thoughts. That is the very reason why Attraction needs a lot of effort. People have to work hard to use the power of autosuggestion, a method of chanting, a habit of writing or scripting, to make Attraction work. But will it always work?

The mind does not want us to attain our ultimate goal. It will permit us to succeed in achieving the pleasure that comes from success and achievement. However, it will stop us from evolving to the peaks of fulfilment and Enlightenment. When we evolve from pleasure to peace, when we still the mind, the mind is at risk of losing its existence. Therefore, who is it that steals our peace of mind? It is the mind itself. The truth is that peace is within. Peace is what we don't have to find. We just have to still the mind. But the mind does not permit this. It continues to grind us with thoughts and destroys our peace. Not only this, it stops us from the process of purification that will lead to the Realization of the truth.

Attraction and Action are not so difficult. But of what use are they if they will take us to the wrong destination? For us to reach our ultimate destination, we need Realization that comes from purification. For us to reach this state of purified thoughts, eliminating toxic thoughts and retaining positive thoughts, we necessarily need to be in a state known as Consciousness.

What is Consciousness? Consciousness is a state of being without thoughts, a state of Awareness, also known as Mindfulness. The world talks about Mindfulness,

Step 7: Be in Consciousness for Purification

meditation and the importance of Awareness. But have we learnt the art of living in Consciousness? Consciousness and the mind are like two sides of a coin. If we are in a disturbed state of mind, then the Consciousness disappears. When we flip the coin of our life to Consciousness, the mind disappears, and we live in peace and bliss. But the mind does not permit us to live in Consciousness. It does not permit us to be in that state of Thoughtlessness because of the risk that the truth will be disclosed, and the mind will cease to exist. Therefore, it will continue to bombard us with thoughts.

How can we overcome the mind and be in Consciousness? The simplest way is to try to spend time in silence and meditation. But the mind will not permit this. It is like a monkey that is constantly jumping from one thought to another. We have to cut the tail of the monkey mind, the 'EY' of the monkey, and make it a 'monk'! The EY of the monkey is Ever-Yearning and Ever-Yelling. The yelling creates so much noise that we are unable to hear the Divine voice within. The yearning creates so many desires that we become prisoners of these thoughts of passion. When we cut the monkey tail EY, cut the Ever-Yelling and Ever-Yearning of the monkey, what is left is a monk. In that state of being a monk, we are free from thought. We reach that state of Thoughtlessness known as Consciousness.

How does one reach this state of Consciousness? Other than being in silence and cutting the tail of the monkey mind, one has to discriminate and choose only PEP and eliminate NEP. One has to reduce the MTR, the Mental Thought Rate. This will lead us into that state of Consciousness. In that state of Consciousness, the mind does not exist. Instead, the intellect shines and discriminates thoughts so that there is purity in our head and not toxic thoughts. Therefore, as long as we are in the mind state, the intellect is subdued. In this state, thoughts pour like rain. They push us down the drain, and they make us suffer again and again. There is no possibility for the intellect to discriminate or purify. Thoughts are gushing like a river in spate. At such a time, it is impossible to construct a dam. It will be washed away. But when there is no river of thoughts, when we still the mind and we are in Consciousness, we can construct the intellect and lock the mind as we remain in Consciousness. In such a state, thoughts will enter one by one, like trolleys in a cable car system. Thoughts will enter like little fishes into the ocean of Consciousness. The intellect will discriminate every thought and this discrimination will lead to purification.

First, we must move from mind to Consciousness. As we block the mind, we must lock it with the intellect. As the intellect discriminates negative from positive, we must work towards purification of our thoughts and our belief systems. Purification means unlearning the myths and realizing the truth. We must question everything we were taught. We must overcome the lie that God lives in the sky. We must question and investigate everything. Only this can take us to the state of purification. We must question our birth and death and what is giving us breath. Unless there is purification in Consciousness, Attraction and Action are of little consequence.

What did we bring with us when we came into this world? What will we take when we depart? Even this body that we consider to be 'me', will be left behind. Therefore, in the seventh step, we take an exit from pleasure that comes from achievement and try to find peace that comes from fulfilment. Ultimately, when we still the mind and there is discrimination with the intellect, we will discover Enlightenment, and the true purpose of our existence. This purification can only happen in Consciousness, when the mind is still. It is purification that will lead to illumination and our ultimate destination. Otherwise, we will continue to be caught in the cycle of Attraction and Action and we will be going in the wrong direction. We will live and die in ignorance, without realizing 'Who am I?' and 'Why am I here?' We will be busy like that little child building a sandcastle on the beach. Ultimately, the child cannot take the castle home. It will be washed away by the waves.

So, purification will start the process of Realization such that we use the power of Attraction and Action to reach our ultimate destination.

'To different minds, the same world is a hell, and a heaven.'
—RALPH WALDO EMERSON

ESSENCE OF STEP 7

BE IN CONSCIOUSNESS FOR PURIFICATION

- The purpose of Attraction and Action is to reach our destination.
- If there is no discrimination, we will be defeated by the mind.
- We must move from a state of mind to a state of Consciousness.
- In Consciousness, we still the mind; we kill the mind!
- In Consciousness, we activate the intellect to discriminate thoughts.
- It is in Consciousness that we can achieve the state of purification and discover our true purpose.
- Without purification and discrimination, there will be Attraction and Action that goes in the wrong direction!
- By living in Consciousness with purification, we will reach our ultimate destination.

STEP 8
LIGHT THE SPARK OF ILLUMINATION FOR REALIZATION

Overcome darkness and spark illumination,
The myths will disappear and there will be Realization.
Then the Law of Attraction will take another direction,
And manifestation will lead to our ultimate Destination.

Action Is the Secret to Attraction

We have reached the eighth step to make Attraction work. After all, we don't want our Attraction to be some distraction that will take us away from our ultimate destination. Who are we and why are we here? Do we ponder these key questions? We have been taught that success is happiness and we keep running after achievement. When will we realize that success is not happiness? Happiness is success. When will we realize that the purpose of success is to be happy? But the paradox is that success creates stress and anxiety. From the time we use Attraction, we are anxious of the result. Then, we get into Action. But still we are trying to be happy. We don't realize the true meaning of happiness. We don't realize that all successful people are not happy, rather, all happy people are successful. Because we don't live in Consciousness and there is no discrimination, our mind makes us blind. We live and die with ignorance, running after attractive things but not attracting the true wealth that we must attain.

Monetary wealth will give us pleasure but ultimately, we will lose our health and one day, the body will die. Then, how have we made use of the magical Law of Attraction, followed up with sincere and earnest Action to take us to the destination that we must reach? Death is certain. Every 'body' must die. Then, why are we running after money, when we know for sure that we cannot take with us even a penny? Isn't it really funny that we are trying

Step 8: Light the Spark of Illumination for Realization

to attract all the worldly pleasures but have forgotten to use the power of visualization for the manifestation of the ultimate? No doubt the secret equation will work. No doubt the combination of Attraction + Action will take us to our destination. But first, should we not use our discrimination to choose the right direction? Should we not flip over from mind to Consciousness? Should not the purification of our thoughts lead us to illumination that will lead to the Realization of the truth?

Therefore, the eighth step challenges us to spark illumination so that there is Realization of the truth. In the previous step, the challenge was to be in Consciousness, not in the mind state. That step is preceded by using discrimination and choosing positive over negative thoughts. Now it is time for Realization. What is the truth? What should we attract? What should be our dreams and goals? Should we just run after achievement that will give pleasure or should we evolve to the second peak of fulfilment that gives peace? When we spark illumination, we will overcome the darkness of ignorance. We will take an exit from the highway of success and choose the road that leads to peace and happiness. Very few people use the Law of Attraction to attract Liberation and Unification—Liberation from the triple suffering on Earth, Liberation from the cycle of rebirth and Unification with the Divine.

When we spark illumination, then one by one, the Realizations dawn upon us. If we use the power of visualization and manifestation for Realization, we move away from the Attraction of material pursuits to the Attraction of spiritual realms that are the real wealth of life. Many of us use the Law of Attraction and manifest success. Alas! We have to leave our success behind. What we earn, others will burn. But we will have to return in another life, carrying our Karma, only to suffer again and again.

However, if we use the Law of Attraction to seek the truth, then this visualization will lead to manifestation of Self-realization. We will discover that we are not this body that will die. We are not the mind that we cannot find. The ego may say 'I' but it's a lie! This is Self-realization. But this cannot happen until we spark illumination. We don't overcome the darkness of ignorance because we are running after money. We are using the Law of Attraction but going in the wrong direction. Even when we reach our destination, we have not arrived. We have to start another journey. The moment we are gone, we will be reborn, and this will go on and on. The goal of life is Liberation, to be free from the cycle of death and rebirth. For this, we need Spiritual Awakening. We need Enlightenment. We need Self-realization. Unless there is purification and illumination, there will be no Realization

Step 8: Light the Spark of Illumination for Realization

that will lead us to Liberation and Unification. The formula can be remembered as PIRLU.

PIRLU teaches us that Purification will lead to Illumination and Realization that will take us to Liberation and Unification. However, for PIRLU to happen, the Law of Attraction needs to play a major part. Only if we can use the power of manifestation with discrimination can we attain Realization.

What is the way to spark illumination? We must go on a quest, and we must put all our beliefs to test. We must question everything that we were taught in school that, in fact, makes us remain fools. We have to unlearn many things that we have learnt. We have to realize that it is a lie that God lives in the sky. We have to awaken to the truth—I am not 'I'. This body will die but I am the Divine Soul. To realize this is my ultimate goal. I am immortal. But this cannot be realized until there is illumination through discrimination. As long as we let the mind make us blind, we will not be in Consciousness and continue to use the equation of Attraction and Action to attain success.

When we spark illumination, we realize that happiness is a state of being, not doing. We realize that peace is the foundation of happiness. Realization reveals that the ultimate peak of happiness is Enlightenment. It is

Liberation from the triple suffering of the body, mind and ego. As long as we are using Attraction to satisfy the desires of our senses and of the mind and ego, ME, we shall never be free. We shall remain prisoners behind the bars of pleasures, possessions and people and we shall suffer. When we spark illumination, there is Realization. The truth is revealed just as the myths that we have grown up with disappear like mist when the sun shines.

The spark of illumination will be like sunshine that will make us realize that the Divine is within. Illumination will take us to Self-realization that we are the SOUL, a Spark Of Unique Life that arrives nine months before our so-called birth date. There is illumination that we arrive on that day of fertilization when two cells become a zygote. Then, after nine months, we arrive on the planet. The spark of illumination will make us realize that we are not this body that will die. We are not the mind that we cannot find! The ego may say 'I' but that is a lie. One day, when the body dies, and there is death as we lose our breath, the Soul, the life within, departs. Illumination reveals that we are that spark. We must use visualization and manifestation to attain this Realization.

Self-realization will lead us to God-realization. When we realize we are the Soul, then the spark of light will reveal that every living creature is a Soul. The Soul is energy. It is power. All Souls come from SIP, the Supreme Immortal

Step 8: Light the Spark of Illumination for Realization

Power, and return to SIP. This is God-realization. God is not God. God is SIP that manifests as every Soul. Unfortunately, most of us don't attain Self-realization and God-realization because we are busy using Attraction for manifestation of success and pleasure. When the power of visualization goes through discrimination and purification, then the spark of illumination will achieve the treasure of life that is greater than any pleasure. We will discover the true purpose of our existence, and this is possible if we use the Laws of Attraction and Action with discrimination.

'When you visualize, then you materialize.'

—DR DENIS WAITLEY

ESSENCE OF STEP 8

LIGHT THE SPARK OF ILLUMINATION FOR REALIZATION

- No doubt that there is power in the Law of Attraction.
- Of what use is Attraction if it takes us to the wrong destination.
- Visualization + Action is a great combination. However, there must be manifestation with discrimination.
- When we spark illumination, then there is Realization.
- When we realize the truth, we overcome the myths.
- We discover the ultimate peak of happiness—Enlightenment.
- Illumination and Realization will lead to Liberation.
- Then we will be free from all misery on Earth and from the cycle of death and rebirth.
- We must spark illumination for Self-realization and God-realization.

STEP 9
REALIZE THAT TWIN KARMA DECIDES OUR DESTINATION

First, realize that twin Karma decides our destination.
Don't protest with desperation and frustration!
Accepting the truth, attain Realization,
And from all Karma be free, get Liberation.

In the journey of life, is everything predetermined, or can we choose our destiny? While we believe that the Law of Attraction works with the secret equation of Attraction + Action, some people believe that life is Karma. Life will unfold depending on our past actions. This busts the Law of Attraction. If everything is predetermined, then how can Attraction work? This is a mystery, and we have to go back to history to realize the truth. No doubt the Law of Attraction is a powerful law and when it is supported by Action, there should be manifestation. However, there is a contradiction. Because of our past actions, we have created Karma. This Karma or past Action should therefore stop Attraction from bearing fruit. Karma or the Law of Action cannot be bypassed. How, then, do the Law of Action and the Law of Attraction work together to unfold as our destiny?

For this, one must understand the Law of Karma. We have already covered this in the fourth step—Get into Action. However, we have more to do with Karma, the Law of Action. Unless we realize twin Karma, we will not understand how the Law of Karma and the Law of Attraction work hand in hand and decide our destination.

Let us understand how the Law of Karma works. Just like a seed we plant must bear the fruit, the deed we plant must unfold as our destiny. Nobody can stop this from happening. When we talk about the Law of Attraction,

Step 9: Realize that Twin Karma Decides Our Destination

there is a contradiction. If our past Karma is going to decide our destination, how can Attraction bypass Karma and lead to a different manifestation? When we understand twin Karma, we find the solution. There is no contradiction. *Let us use the analogy of driving a car on the road. The car is in your hands. You can go left or right, forward or backward, slow or fast. But can you change the road? The road is already laid. It is like our past Karma.* We can't change what is going to unfold as per our past deeds but we can plant fresh seeds with our present Action. When we use the power of Attraction and let visualization create new Action, then we can use the combination of past Karma and Attraction to achieve our destination. Some things will happen as per past Karma. There is no doubt. But we are not like puppets who are living with our wings tied with strings. We have been blessed with the power of discrimination. We have our willpower and intellect to choose. We can use thought and attract what we wish. But we must work along with Karma. We must realize that it is twin Karma that will decide our destination.

Those who blindly pursue the Law of Attraction, sometimes find a roadblock on their path. They are zooming forward in the direction of their dreams and goals but suddenly, something unavoidable happens and it creates a bottleneck in their Attraction. Because they don't understand twin Karma, they protest and reject.

They cry and ask, 'Why?' Those who realize the truth of twin Karma, learn not only to accept but also to surrender. They do their best but realize that it is a combination of past Action and Attraction that will decide our destination. Those who realize the truth of twin Karma have no confusion. They live their life using both Attraction and Action as a combination, keeping in mind past Karma that will unfold along the way.

If there is past Karma, and then present Attraction and Action create new Karma, how will there be Liberation from this cycle? This is a key question for those who are seeking the ultimate goal of Liberation. They don't just seek pleasure from Attraction while they surrender to twin Karma and move in that direction to their predetermined destination. They probe further as to how they can use Attraction for Realization of the way to Liberation.

What is our ultimate goal? Is it just Attraction and Action? Is it going round and round in the merry-go-round of life? Is it to be born and then to learn, to earn, to burn and to return? This is what Karma does. The cycle goes on and on! But attaining Salvation or Liberation, *Nirvana* or *Moksha*, means transcending twin Karma. It means using Attraction for the Realization of the truth. One can use Attraction for Enlightenment or Spiritual Awakening. Then one realizes that I am not

Step 9: Realize that Twin Karma Decides Our Destination

this body that will die, and I am not the mind and ego, 'ME'. I am the Divine Soul. This Realization reveals that Karma doesn't belong to us. It belongs to the illusory mind and ego that is so busy with Attraction and Action. Finally, when the body dies, the illusory mind and ego carry the outstanding unsettled Karma and it returns in reincarnation. We do not reach the ultimate destination of Unification with the Divine.

However, if we use the power of visualization with discrimination, if we move from mind to Consciousness and use the same power of Attraction to seek the truth and to seek Liberation, then we would have the Realization of how to be free from twin Karma. We will be awakened that we are the Divine Soul. Then we achieve our ultimate goal.

However, to reach this far in the journey of life, we have to evolve. We have to grow through Attraction and Action. We have to climb from the peak of achievement to the plateau of fulfilment. Finally, we want Enlightenment, for this leads to Liberation from the cycle of death and rebirth. But to get to this state, we need to use the Law of Attraction, in combination with Action. We must use this secret equation not just for the manifestation of riches but for the manifestation of Unification with the Supreme. This is the purpose and the goal of human life.

Those who blindly use the Law of Attraction, enamoured by pleasures and possessions of the material world, will use the power of visualization but reach the wrong destination. Because they don't understand the Law of Karma—the Law of Action—and don't realize that it is twin Karma that will decide their destination, they often reach a state of desperation and frustration, when Attraction doesn't work. Because they have not understood twin Karma, they have not realized that there is a mysterious factor that is beyond Action and Attraction. What is it?

Man believes that there are three factors that are responsible for the result of his Action. The three factors are the quality of his equipment, the method that he follows, and the efficiency with which he works. For any Action, these three factors together create the result. If different farmers use the same method of farming, with the same plough, seeds and fertilizers, on the same farmland and work with the same efficiency, the result should be the same. However, the results may vary. How is this possible? This is because there is a fourth factor that controls the results of all Actions, a factor beyond man's understanding. The fourth unknown factor is our past Karma. This puts to rest why there is disruption in the equation of Attraction and Action.

First, one must realize twin Karma to understand how life unfolds. Then, one must go beyond twin Karma and

Step 9: Realize that Twin Karma Decides Our Destination

be free from Karma. One must attain the Realization that I am not the body that does the Action. I am not the mind and ego, ME, that causes the Attraction. I am the Divine Soul that is not bound by any Karma or Action. This Realization leads to Liberation and to the next step in the journey of life.

'It is not our past Karma that decides our luck,
It is Twin Karma that will determine what we pluck!'

—AiR

ESSENCE OF STEP 9

REALIZE THAT TWIN KARMA DECIDES OUR DESTINATION

- Life is not a simple equation of Attraction + Action.
- Sometimes, there is a disruption and we don't understand why.
- Things don't happen because of our past Karma, deeds that have already been done.
- Life is a combination of past Action and present Action.
- Everything happens as per twin Karma. This decides our destination.
- While Attraction + Action works, a mysterious factor can cause a roadblock in reaching our destination.
- We must realize twin Karma and live with acceptance and surrender.
- Finally, we must go beyond twin Karma and attain Liberation, freedom from all Karma.
- We must realize we are not the body and mind responsible for Action and Attraction.
- We are the Soul. This Realization will lead to Liberation.

STEP 10
ACHIEVE THE GOAL OF LIBERATION AND DIVINE UNIFICATION

Of what use are the Laws of Attraction and Action,
If ultimately, we suffer and return in reincarnation?
We must use Visualization for
Illumination and Realization,
And attain the ultimate goal of
Liberation and Unification.

Action Is the Secret to Attraction

What is the ultimate goal of our life? We are so busy doing so many things that don't matter that there is no time to focus on things that matter. We are alive but one day, the body will die. We know nothing about death and afterlife. Instead of understanding the purpose of our existence, who we are, and why we are here, we are trying to change the world which is just a stage. We are like actors who come and go. This world is just a show. We know this but we don't take this into account before we get into that cycle of Attraction and Action. How many of us have a clear direction? How many of us have discovered the answers to two of life's most important questions:

1. Who am I?
2. Why am I here?

We are born but do we know what brought us to Earth? What caused this human birth? Did we choose our mother and our father, our nationality, our gender, our religion? We did not! Who chose? Why is a child born blind? Is it because God is cruel or unkind? Why is somebody born in a palace and somebody else in a slum? Is it some random magic or is there any logic? What makes this Earth rotate precisely once every 24 hours and how does it revolve around the sun in 365¼ days? We human beings are so intelligent that we have discovered all this but we have not discovered who

Step 10: Achieve the Goal of Liberation and Divine Unification

has created this universe. We talk of a God but we don't know who, where or what is God. We come to the planet and spend a quarter of our life learning. Then the next quarter, we spend earning. After we learn and earn, we are so lost that our life doesn't seem to have any meaning or purpose. It becomes like a circus and we become clowns, jumping up and down. Then one day, at death, the body will be either buried or burned or cremated. Thereafter, we will return. We will be born again, and this cycle will go on and on.

In this journey of about a 100 years, the lifespan of a human being, we are so busy *doing* that there is no time for *being*. We don't reflect and introspect on the purpose of our existence. We all want pleasure. We don't want pain and we are taught that success is happiness. To be successful, we learn the Law of Attraction. Some of us are fortunate. We successfully use visualization for the manifestation of our dreams. But then, ultimately, whatever we earn, others will burn. We will return. Is this what we seek? We try to climb the peak but we don't realize that the ultimate peak is the cliff called death. Nothing will belong to us. Nobody will be ours. Don't we see that when death places its icy hands on us, we are nothing.

We start with nothing. We try to become something. We achieve everything but in the end, nothing will be ours!

Our purpose is to realize the truth. We need illumination so that we are free from the darkness of ignorance in which we suffer. Every human being suffers pain of the body, misery of the mind and agony of the ego. Our goal is to be free from this triple suffering on Earth, just as it is to be free from the cycle of death and rebirth. Our goal is Liberation also known as Salvation or *Nirvana* or *Moksha*. Our ultimate goal is Unification with the Divine. This is the purpose of human existence. Unfortunately, we are so busy in the Attraction of wealth that ultimately, we lose our health and before we realize who we are, in reality, we die! Then, we return to Earth in another birth.

Only if we use the power of Attraction with Action, then we can use visualization for the Realization of the truth. We can overcome ignorance with illumination and achieve the ultimate goal of Liberation. Just as we use Attraction for success and achievement, we can use the same visualization for Spiritual Awakening and Enlightenment. This is our ultimate goal, to realize we are the Divine Soul. But unfortunately, we get caught in thought and we go round and round in the merry-go-round of life, only to repeat the cycle of arrival and departure.

Of course, we should be happy. But when will we realize that pleasure is not happiness? When will we evolve from the peak of achievement to fulfilment and ultimately,

Step 10: Achieve the Goal of Liberation and Divine Unification

Enlightenment? When will we discover what Attraction should be used for and what should be the direction of our Action? No doubt Attraction is very powerful but if our visualization is in the wrong direction, we will not reach our ultimate destination.

In the tenth step, we must use discrimination to achieve the ultimate goal of Liberation from this world and Unification with the Divine. We must realize that with death, which is certain, one of two things will happen. In most cases, the body will die, and the mind and ego—ME, will carry its Karma, its unsettled Action, and return to Earth in a new body. This journey of coming and going can have Attraction and Action but it will not lead to our ultimate goal of Liberation. In rare cases, when there is illumination and Realization that we are not the body or mind but we are the Divine Soul, there will be Liberation from this cycle of coming and going.

How can one attain this ultimate goal of Liberation? It doesn't happen by magic. There is a clear logic. One has to follow a step-by-step method. One has to go on a quest and use the power of discrimination. Here, one can use the Law of Attraction by planting seeds of thought and using deeds or Actions for the Realization of the truth. Instead of wasting our life running after achievement, which is temporary or ephemeral, we can invest our life in seeking Enlightenment, which will lead us to the ultimate goal of Liberation. It all depends on our choice, what we attract in our life. If we attract material success, we will achieve that. But if we want to attract God in our life, then that deep yearning for the Divine can lead us through the process of Self-realization to God-realization. For this, we can use the Laws of Attraction and Action. We must be in Consciousness, using our intellect for discrimination.

Do we realize that we human beings are the only blessed ones who have a fully developed intellect and the willpower to discriminate and choose? A dog or a frog, a cat or a rat cannot attain Liberation and Unification. They live and they die. But they cannot discriminate. But you and I can and we must. If we don't, then we lose this opportunity of being human. One day, we will go and if we don't get to know, 'Who am I and why am I here?' then we will just live and die and by not attaining Liberation from the cycle of death and rebirth, shall again return to this cosmic show. But if we start today, and we use the power of visualization, the Law of Attraction, and back it with dedication and devotion through persistent Action, without any distraction or distortion created by the mind, we can arrive at our destination—Liberation. We will be free from all misery and attain Unification with the Divine. Realization will reveal that we are the Divine Soul, the Spark of Unique Life, and the Soul is

Step 10: Achieve the Goal of Liberation and Divine Unification

none other than SIP, the Supreme Immortal Power, that the world calls, God.

The tenth step in the journey of Attraction is to achieve the goal of Liberation. We must evolve beyond Attraction of ordinary things and use visualization for Realization of the truth. If we use the secret equation of Attraction + Action, with discrimination, we will attain the ultimate goal of Unification with the Divine. At death, when the physical body dies, we, the Soul, will become one with SIP. This is our ultimate goal, and we must not let this slip.

> *'Moksha comes after Mukti. From Rebirth it is Liberation. In that moment of death, there is Divine Unification.'*
>
> —AiR

ESSENCE OF STEP 10

ACHIEVE THE GOAL OF LIBERATION AND DIVINE UNIFICATION

- No doubt the Law of Attraction is very powerful. But what are we seeking?
- If we use visualization just to earn, then one day we will be gone, and others will burn what we earn.
- 'What is the purpose of our life?' We must get this Realization.
- Our ultimate purpose is to be free from misery on Earth and the cycle of rebirth.
- We must use Attraction and visualization for the Realization of the truth.
- We must realize that we are not the body or mind. We are the Soul. To realize this, is our goal.
- With the right thought and Action, we can use our discrimination for illumination.
- Ultimately, we will be free from the cycle of death and rebirth, and we shall not return to Earth.
- We can use Attraction and Action for Liberation and Unification with the Divine.

STEP 11
CONVERT INFORMATION
TO A TRANSFORMATION

*If you want the ultimate goal of Liberation,
Then convert information to a transformation.
If you don't use discrimination for purification,
You will never reach your destination.*

Action Is the Secret to Attraction

The eleventh step in this journey of Attraction is not just getting into Action with Attraction. It is the ability to use visualization effectively through discrimination. One has to convert information to a transformation.

We have so much information that we are zapped. This world is full of attractions and distractions and very few amongst us are able to achieve our true purpose. Very few reach the ultimate goal of Realization, Liberation, Unification. How can we do that? We have to convert information and reach the level of transformation. In fact, we need a metamorphosis that is irreversible. For this, going through these 12 steps is very important. The Law of Attraction is very powerful. But it needs Action to complete the equation. However, even if we complete the equation but go in the wrong direction, we can't reach our destination. Therefore, we have to convert the information and then light the fire of Attraction.

> *'Whatever we plant in our subconscious mind and nourish with repetition and emotion will one day become a reality.'*
>
> —EARL NIGHTINGALE

Information is either true or false. We can either believe the lie that God lives in the sky or we can dissect the information to find out 'Who am I?' When there is

Step 11: Convert Information to a Transformation

Realization that I am not 'I', I am not the body that will die, I am not the mind that I cannot find, the ego that says 'I' is a lie, then we have taken information and used discrimination for the Realization of the truth. Without this Realization, Attraction and Action are meaningless. They are just temporary. But if we are able to discriminate, we can initiate that journey of transformation. If we don't convert information, then we will just be following the herd. Our wings will be tied with strings, and we will not fly like a bird to ask, investigate and realize the truth.

The truth is, there is too much information. There are too many theories. There are innumerable religions, theologies and philosophies. People are confused! What is right? What is wrong? We need crystallization of information, after purification. We must eliminate impurities, myths, superstitions, rituals and dogmas. Once we cleanse the junk, we must contemplate like a monk. Only then will the right information lead to a transformation. If we use the wrong information, the power of Attraction will manifest as a wrong destiny. Of what use is it to use Attraction that will not lead to our ultimate goal? Our ultimate goal is Realization and Liberation. It is transformation from who we think we are to who we truly are. Man doesn't realize that his body is just a costume. He is the Divine Soul. He is the manifestation of God. But man thinks that he is made of flesh and bones and he doesn't realize that he is the Divine that dwells within. This is man's greatest sin and unless man overcomes fake or wrong information, he cannot reach that state of transformation, which will eventually lead to a metamorphosis.

We must take the help of an Enlightened Master to help us discriminate and guide us in the right path. Without this, we will just be going round in circles. An Awakened Master has himself gone through a transformation and so he will guide us in the right direction. We can continue the journey of life without such a Master, also known as guru, one who takes us from *Gu* to *Ru*, from darkness to light, but it is just like trying to become a champion in sports without a qualified coach. Therefore, we must seek advice from an Enlightened Master. We will then be able to understand the Divine Laws of both Attraction and Action and go through the transformation that will lead to a metamorphosis.

What is the transformation that one needs? The Realization—I am not this. I am that. I am not this body. I am not the mind and ego. I am that Divine Power that manifests as the Soul. This is crystallization of the right information. This will lead to the ultimate transformation. Man will be able to experience God as SIP, the Supreme Immortal Power, in one and all. He

Step 11: Convert Information to a Transformation

will be able to see God in all, love God in all and serve God in all. For this, man needs to use the Law of Attraction with the right Action. He needs illumination that will lead him to Realization, and this cannot happen until his information goes through purification. Only then can man experience much desired transformation. If man is so busy using the power of Attraction for success and achievement, then where is the chance for him to reach that state of Enlightenment, which needs so much dedication and devotion in this journey of Realization.

Most of us don't experience this transformation. We don't realize the truth of who we are and why we are here. We live and die without discovering, 'Who am I?' and without going through any kind of transformation, let alone metamorphosis. Unfortunately, we are glued to modern technology which spreads so much misinformation that we get confused about the truth! Instead of living in peace and bliss, our life is full of unhappiness. Have we ever thought why? It is because we permit the mind to create stress and worry for the things that we cannot find. We start to use Attraction to achieve pleasure, which is not true happiness. Ultimately, we become unhappy. Although there is a formula to manifest what we like, we manifest the wrong things because we are enamoured with the wrong information. So, we don't experience the magical transformation that liberates us from misery and sorrow. We just jump from yesterday to tomorrow, without enjoying the present moment in bliss.

> *'Every single second is an opportunity to change your life because in any moment, you can change the way you feel.'*
>
> —RHONDA BYRNE

While we must discover the Law of Attraction and use visualization, we must be careful not to be misguided with misinformation. It is so important to go through all the steps and use discrimination. This precious journey of life will be over one day and if there is no Realization, we will end up in reincarnation. However, if we convert information and realize the truth, there will be a transformation. We will be liberated from the cycle and united with the Supreme.

It's time to stop and first look at all the information before we put the power of Attraction into Action. Before we use visualization, let us use our discrimination, let us choose the right path in this precious human birth that will make us free from the cycle of death and rebirth. The entire process is not complicated. But the mind can bombard us with thoughts and we can be caught in negative toxic emotions. Then we are doomed! We will never discover that we are the Soul and never reach our ultimate goal.

Step 11: Convert Information to a Transformation

Do you want a transformation? Then take a pause! Check all your information before you get into Action.

'We do not need magic to transform our world; we carry all the power we need inside ourselves already.'

—J.K. ROWLING

ESSENCE OF STEP 11

CONVERT INFORMATION TO A TRANSFORMATION

- No doubt the Law of Attraction is very powerful but it is also dangerous.
- If we do not discriminate information, we cannot reach our destination.
- Therefore, before we put Attraction into Action, we must stop and discriminate.
- We must remove all misinformation, myths, superstitions, rituals and dogmas.
- We must take the help of an enlightened master to help us discriminate and guide us in the right path.
- Finally, after discrimination and purification, our goal is to convert that information into transformation.
- If there is no transformation, we will suffer on Earth and return in reincarnation.
- Attraction and Action are meaningless if there is no transformation.
- We must use the Divine Laws for a metamorphosis.

STEP 12
ELIMINATE CONFUSION AND GET TO THE CONCLUSION

Our goal is to reach our ultimate destination,
To attain liberation after there is realization.
But for this, first, we must eliminate all confusion,
Only then will we get to the right conclusion.

What is life all about? Is it not like a movie, a drama, a show? Are we not like actors who come to the Earth stage and go? If we don't realize that life has a purpose, it will just be like a circus. We will just live like a clown, who is jumping up and down.

'All that we are is a result of what we have thought.'

—THE BUDDHA

What is the purpose of this human birth? Why did we come to Earth? Is it just to attract money, wealth, name, fame and then, ultimately leave it all behind? The story of money is very funny because we can't take a penny after we die! Yet, we have so much passion, and we get into Action and use Attraction to create wealth, which will never belong to us. What we earn, others will burn, and we will then return on Earth, and the cycle will go on! Isn't it time to eliminate all confusion and get to the conclusion? This is the twelfth step in the journey of Attraction.

No doubt, Attraction is a powerful law. But of what use is Attraction if it is distraction from our ultimate destination? What is the point if we just live and die and we don't understand why? When something goes wrong, we look up at the sky and cry. Then, one day, we will

Step 12: Eliminate Confusion and Get to the Conclusion

die and when we return to Earth in a rebirth, we will continue in that cycle of Attraction and Action. If there is no Realization of the truth, if there is no Liberation from this cycle, if there is no Unification with the Divine, then we have wasted our power of discrimination and the magic of visualization. Isn't it important that we stop and get a clear direction? Otherwise, our passion, our obsession, will be a complete waste. We are trying to find the right way to do the wrong thing. What is the point?

If we are traumatized by this life drama and we don't understand that it is Karma, we will never attain *Moksha*, the ultimate goal of life that makes us realize that we are not the body, mind and ego—we are the Divine Soul. How will we get to the conclusion? The only way is to eliminate confusion.

In this journey of Attraction, our biggest challenge is to overcome the mind, the mind which we cannot find but the rascal that still makes us blind. As long as we let the monkey mind jump into yesterday and tomorrow, our life will be full of misery and sorrow. If we want to get to the conclusion, we have to eliminate all confusion caused by the mind. We have to eliminate the junk and live like a monk. The monkey mind must be tamed. We have to cut its tail, the 'EY' of the monkey—Ever-Yelling and Ever-Yearning. Then we can live like a 'monk' and get to the conclusion. As long as we are in the monkey mind state, there will always be confusion because the mind is drilling us and killing us with up to 50 thoughts a minute. Then how can we reach our destination?

What is the ultimate purpose of life? To find out 'Who am I?' and 'Why am here?' Without this Realization, Attraction will take us into confusion. We must first bring in discrimination to overcome ignorance. As long as we believe in the myths we have grown up with, we will never realize the truth. To eliminate confusion, we must get to the root. There, we will get to the conclusion as to what should be our visualization, our Attraction, our Action. No doubt the magic of Attraction and Action, the secret equation, will take us in that direction. But what if the direction is wrong? Do we want to reach the wrong destination? What is the destination? Every 'body' has to die. But when we die and we don't realize 'Who am I?' then this journey of life will be a waste. We lived in haste to visualize and attract our dreams and passion. But all our Actions went down the drain. All the Attraction was in vain, for we have to come back again and again and suffer the pain. It's time to stop, eliminate confusion and get to the conclusion.

Without Realization of the truth, we can use the power of visualization and Attraction but we will never reach our ultimate destination. It is time to question everything. It is time to ask and investigate. It is time to realize the

Step 12: Eliminate Confusion and Get to the Conclusion

truth. It is time to overcome our greatest sin—the sin of ignorance that conceals the truth that we are a Divine manifestation, the sin that projects the myths and leads us into a passion for Attraction of material possessions.

We all want to be happy. But will success and achievement that come from Attraction give us eternal bliss? When will we realize the paradox? Success is not success. Success is not happiness. Success is meant to create bliss but it creates stress and unhappiness. Unfortunately, we were taught the wrong things in school and so we remain fools! Let us stop and try to discriminate between the right and wrong information. Let us dissect and eliminate all myths and superstitions and reach the conclusion as we wipe out all confusion. It is time to get into Action, to use the Law of Attraction but only after we have reached the conclusion!

We all have this powerful tool in our hand, the tool of the human computer. We have the gift of being born human and the precious gift of the intellect is only given to us to discriminate, to realize the truth and to be liberated. At our disposal we have the Law of Attraction and the Law of Action. But without discrimination, we will have our passion and obsession that will give us success, although when we die, we will return in reincarnation. This is not our ultimate goal. Our ultimate goal is to realize we are the Soul and to attain Liberation from this world of misery and sorrow. We must attain Unification with the Divine. If we use these 12 steps effectively, we can use the power of visualization with discrimination to reach our destination. All this is only possible if we discover the Law of Attraction and within it, the powerful Law of Action. If we use this secret equation of Attraction + Action, then we will reach our ultimate destination.

'Manifestation without action is only a wish.'
—NANETTE MATHEWS

ESSENCE OF STEP 12

ELIMINATE CONFUSION AND
GET TO THE CONCLUSION

- No doubt the Law of Attraction is very powerful and it will take us to our destination.
- If we use the secret equation of Attraction + Action, it will lead to manifestation.
- But if our life is full of confusion, we will go in the wrong direction.
- Unless we eliminate all the junk and live like a monk, there will be no discrimination.
- We have to tame the monkey mind and cut its tail EY—Ever-Yelling and Ever-Yearning.
- We have to get rid of all myths, all dogmas and all superstitions.
- Once we eliminate all confusion, we will reach our conclusion.
- Realization will lead to Liberation and Divine Unification. We will attain our ultimate goal of realizing that we are the Divine Soul.
- All this is possible with the equation—Attraction + Action, used with discrimination.

AFTERWORD

I started with nothing but with the Law of Attraction,
I became something as I used visualization,
I achieved everything, adding Action to Attraction,
Only to realize we are nothing, without Realization.

For 25 years, I used the Law of Attraction to make my dreams come true. I used visualization and autosuggestion, and there was a manifestation of my dreams and goals. In fact, I had a unique method of creating my 'obsession statement'. People talk of mission statement and vision statement. I was so passionate that I would not just write down a plan of how I would make things happen, rather I would use the power of visualization that would drive me to Action. The result—I moved from peak to peak, from one success to another! I had inadvertently learnt that success doesn't come from either hard work or smart work. It comes from both. I had discovered that success doesn't come from Attraction or Action. It comes from the combination, the secret equation of Attraction + Action. Though I am writing this book now, I have been implementing this principle for decades. Now, I have formulated it into a 12-step method to make Attraction work.

The 12-step method that I have listed, covers not only the Laws of Attraction and Action but also goes beyond. It covers the very essence of our life and reincarnation, and shows us the way to Liberation, through Realization. Each step may seem to rhyme but every rhyme is worth the dime. These steps will make one reach the top. I used every step that is mentioned in this book to reach where I am today. I have evolved beyond the peak of achievement where I was for over 25 years, lived on the plateau of fulfilment for about eight years and experienced the peace and bliss of Enlightenment for the last 10 years. Therefore, when I talk about the Law of Attraction and what lies within, I go deep inside the journey of life and the purpose of existence.

Today, I have reached my ultimate destination and it is my vision to help people have a new vision. No doubt, discovering the Law of Attraction is the key to open the door to this journey. But if we don't understand how to use the power of visualization and how to make manifestation work, then we will just live and then

Afterword

die, without reaching our destination. We will lose this treasure called life, because we did not choose to get into Action, the engine that makes Attraction work.

Many people use the secret equation Attraction + Action but don't reach their ultimate destination. It is unfortunate that we are going in the wrong direction. There is so much misinformation that we are unable to use our gift of discrimination. When I learnt that our biggest enemy was the mind, I went in search of the mind. Instead, I found Consciousness. My Attraction moved in a new direction, and I was blessed to experience purification of information. I separated the myths from the truth and on 31 August 2014 is when I got the spark of illumination that the world calls Realization.

For the last 10 years, I have been making every possible effort to help people not just discover the Law of Attraction and how within it lies the Law of Action but more importantly, to reach the ultimate goal of Realization and Liberation. My goal is to touch, trigger and transform people, to help them start with Attraction, get into Action and experience a transformation. We all have the same opportunity, and we can use our intellect to discriminate, or we can just let this opportunity pass by as we seek pleasure and then die one day. We have to make a conscious effort to still the mind and kill the mind. I did that after I flipped from NEP to PEP, from

Action Is the Secret to Attraction

negative to positive, from mind to Consciousness.

Then I discovered that everything unfolding in this life drama was as per Karma. I became free from trauma. When I further studied about all this, I discovered that there are two kinds of Karma. One, that causes our birth and another, what we do after we come to Earth. Both Karma merge together to become the cause of all effects, which become a combined Action that causes reaction, leading to the destiny that unfolds.

Not everybody is blessed to go through these 12 steps. Even the first step of the Law of Attraction is not used by one and all. Only a small part of humanity discovers the Law of Attraction, and a smaller part puts this Law of Attraction into Action. A very tiny fraction reaches the ultimate destination of Liberation. However, I am grateful to be blessed for my awakening and I know for sure that anybody who wants to attain Self-realization can use Attraction to achieve this. Of course, we have to follow all the 12 steps but there is no doubt that if our direction is right, we will reach our destination, with the Laws of Attraction and Action.

*'You become what you think about most,
but you also attract what you think about most.'*

—JOHN ASSARAF

MY 'GIVING' JOURNEY

*'I had nothing, but whatever I got,
I started to give.
The more I gave, the more I got!
What a magical way to live!'*

No doubt the world saw me as a successful person because whatever I touched turned to gold. There was success and more success. But the world did not understand the secret of my success. To me, the secret was simple; it was based on the universal law of Karma: *As you sow, so shall you reap. What you give is what you will get.*

From my first success, whatever I made, I gave a lot of it away. Somehow, I did not selfishly hoard and store my wealth. I don't even know why I kept giving, because it started when I was a child. Today, I feel grateful that I was blessed to give, for I realize it is in giving that we receive. One thing is sure, my success was fuelled by my giving. The deeds of charity and service undoubtedly became the seeds that created the roots of success, the shoots of prosperity and the fruits of wealth and happiness.

I gave to everybody I could, not just to my family and friends but to strangers as well. I would help anyway I could. I would help old people cross the street. I would share my meals with those who worked in our household. When I started earning, I shared my income with the poor and the underprivileged who were sleeping on the streets. So, what I am sharing is not some theory. It comes from my personal experience that the more I gave, the more I received. In fact, I received much more than what I gave away.

My giving continued as my success hit the skies. I made millions, but I also gave away millions. It had become an automatic circle of my life. I experienced great joy in giving and this inspired me to give more and more.

From my initial business success, I set up a humanitarian trust. Our goal was to pick up people from the streets and put them back on their feet. Some people had not eaten for days. They would have died. It was through Divine intervention that the team in our Trust, which was full of people with compassion and humanitarian hearts, was led to serve the destitute and the downtrodden. We found beggars on the street, and we set up small shops for them and provided them with merchandise to sell so that they did not have to beg for a living. When houses were ravaged by rain, we would reconstruct the roofs of the houses of the poor. We did anything and everything possible to serve the needy.

I was barely 30 when I started a weekly 'Giving Day'. Every Monday, I would sit and wait for people to come to me with their problems and their needs. I would personally listen to their stories and try to find a way to help them. We were able to help thousands of people live with dignity and respect. We gave medicines to the poor, just as we funded their surgeries and treatment.

As we did this, we realized that the existing charitable homes had limitations. They had too many conditions for admission and did not admit all those who needed support. For instance, we found a child who was both mentally and physically challenged. Since we supported and sponsored several charitable institutions, we approached them for that child's admission. One of them said that they could only take care of the physically challenged, while another stated that they could take care of only those who were mentally challenged. We were left helpless and hopeless. We then decided to set up our own humanitarian home. We bought a piece of land and constructed a 100-bed home. We admitted people who could not be admitted to any charitable institutions. A poor maidservant had a child, and she approached a charitable mission. They refused to accept the child until she promised never to see her child again. Sobbing and crying, she brought the child to us.

Hundreds of such cases, of people who are turned away at other charitable homes, still come to us. We admit them in one of our three homes. We have about 700 people staying with us. We look after them, providing food, clothing, medicines and love and care. They are our family!

Where did the money come from? I don't even know. All I know is that when we wanted the money, it was always there. There was never a time when we were short of funds. Even today, we spend millions to serve the poor, and while there are several supporters and donors who regularly contribute to this mammoth but humble cause, it was 'giving', for sure, that led to us receiving the funds and the support we needed to make all this possible. While I gave a lot to those who needed it, I also wanted to do something for God. At that time, I was deeply religious, and my faith in my God made me build a 65-foot statue of my God—Lord Shiva. Little did

I realize that trying to give to my God's temple would become another source of getting resources to do even bigger charitable projects.

The 'Giving' journey has never stopped since then. I have evolved from a religious to a spiritual person, and my transformation has led to my metamorphosis. I continue to lead the charitable and other organizations I have set up. But personally what I now give to others are my Realizations. I give away books, just as I give away a lot of innovative merchandise that can help people realize the truth about life. While I can't 'give' Enlightenment to others, I give talks and provide answers to questions that can help people on the ultimate journey of Self-realization, Enlightenment, Liberation and Unification with the Divine. This is the mission of my life.

If I reflect upon my life, I am grateful for all the blessings I have received. I realize that in the beginning, it was the law of Karma that was working. But I went beyond doing good Karma to becoming a *Karma Yogi*. I realized that every creature, whether a human being or a beast, was nothing but a manifestation of the Divine. Now, I experience God as SIP, or the Supreme Immortal Power in one and all and so, I serve not the bodies that are suffering, but the temple that houses the Soul that is none other than the Supreme Immortal Power. This makes me a *Karma Yogi*, one who is ever united with the Divine through acts of good deeds or Karma.

Right from the beginning, I knew nothing is mine, that we come empty-handed and we leave empty-handed. I was blessed to live with detachment and even today, I try to give away as much as I can. I even realize that it is not me who is giving, these hands are not mine. I am just an instrument of the Divine. It is the Divine will that causes the 'giving' through my hands. It may appear that I give, but in reality, all 'giving' is that of the Divine. If only we realize this, and we live and give, we can not only enjoy the blessings of the Supreme Lord, which will liberate us from the triple suffering on earth—pain of the body, misery of the mind and agony of the ego—but ultimately, we will be united with the Divine as we are liberated from the cycle of rebirth.

We may pray to a God, but we do not realize that God is not God. God is SIP, the Supreme Immortal Power, residing in you and me. We are ignorant about this truth and thus refrain from giving while living. If only we realize that we are nothing, and that we are all part of that one SIP, we will give everything away. Somehow, the body, mind and ego keep us trapped in ignorance and we do not realize that we come with nothing and we will go with nothing. The ego makes us believe that I am 'I' and this is mine. I was lucky to realize that nothing is mine. Everything is thine! Even I am thine! With this

Divine revelation, my life has evolved to where it is today. I hope that I continue to give as I live and when that day comes when it is time to go and I hear the death whistle blow, I should have given away everything that I have. My aspiration is to give before I am gone, so that I become one with the Divine and I am not reborn.

'When it is time to go, and I hear the death whistle blow,
May I have given away all that seemed to be mine,
This is my prayer, O Divine!'

'IF WE DON'T GIVE, WE DON'T LIVE.'—AiR

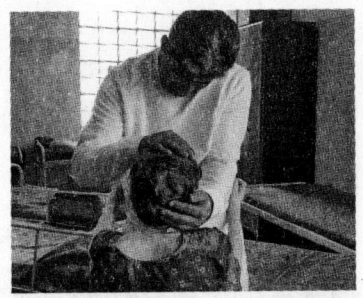
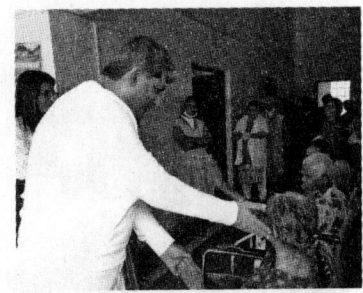

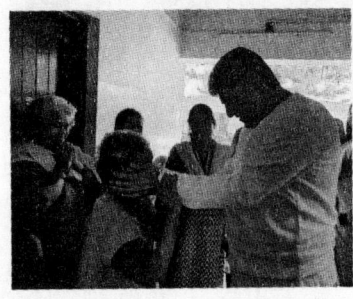
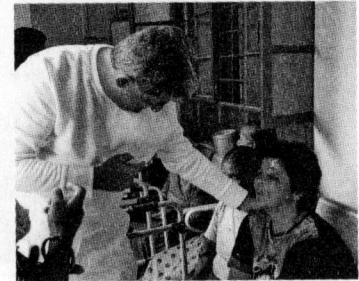

TO AiR, SERVICE TO HUMANITY IS PRAYER TO GOD.

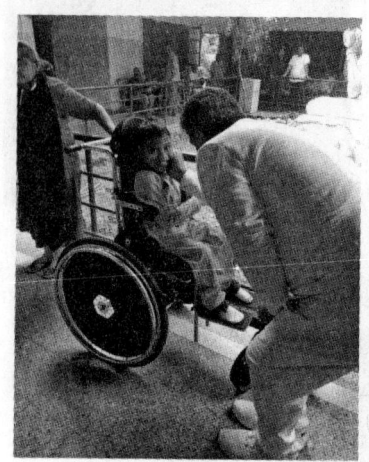
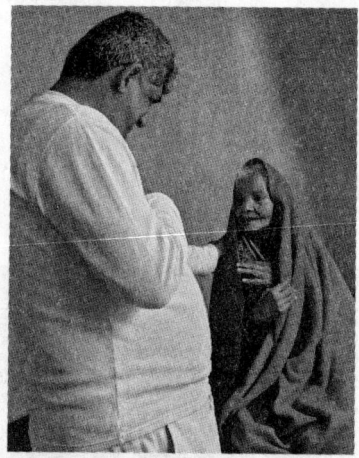
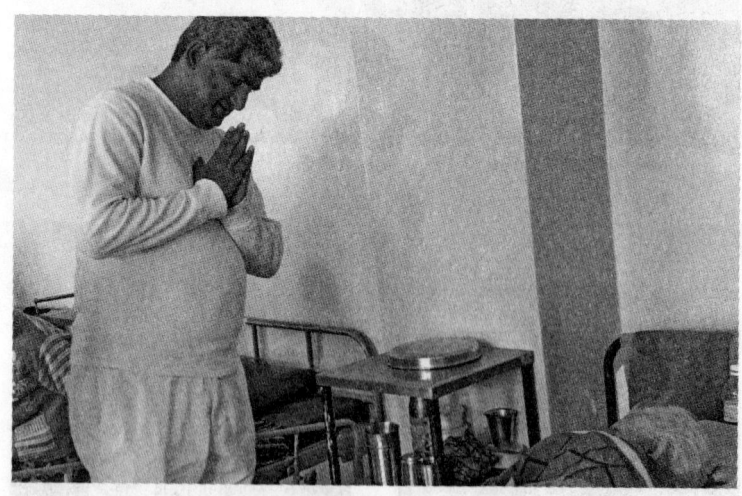

'WHEN WE LOVE THE POOR, THE DESTITUTE,
WE ARE LOVING GOD.'—AiR

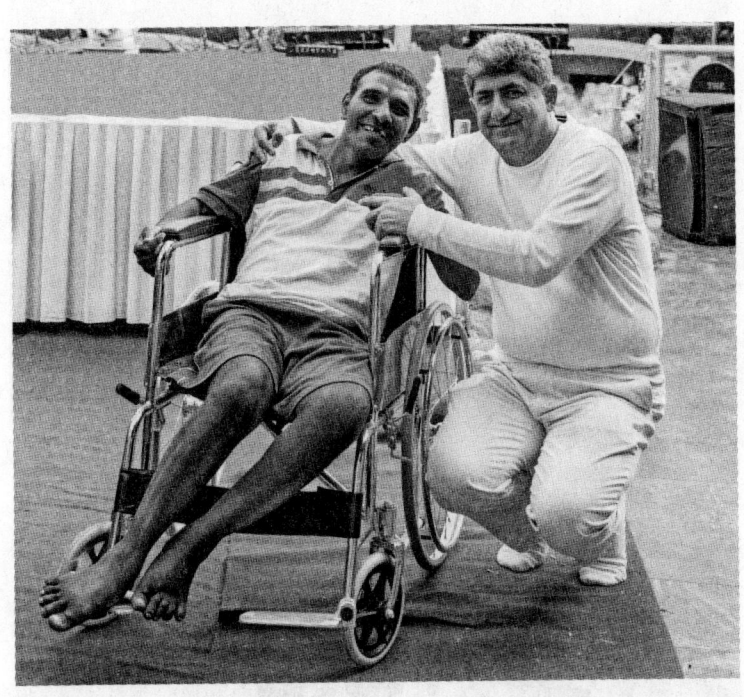

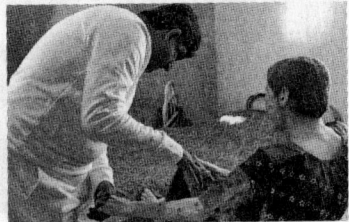

AiR WITH HIS FAMILY OF 700. SHIVA WAS BROUGHT TO AiR HUMANITARIAN HOMES 30 YEARS AGO.

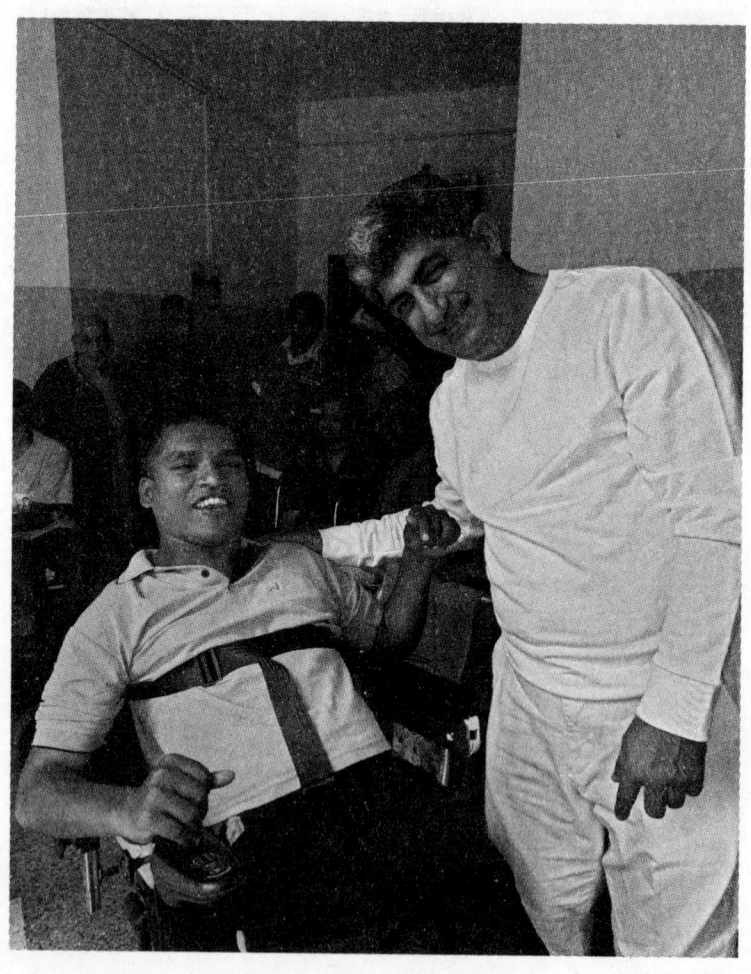

LIST OF BOOKS BY AiR

1. Talaash
2. 3 Peaks of Happiness
3. My Guru, My Mentor, My God on Earth
4. I Will Never Die, Death Is Not "The End"
5. Death Is Not "The End", Death Is "Liberation"
6. I Am Not I. Who Am I?
7. The Mind Is a Rascal
8. A Cosmic Drama
9. Who Is God? Where Is God? What Is God?
10. The A to Z of Karma
11. Who Are You & Why Are You Here?
12. The 4th Factor
13. Be Happy in the NOW!
14. Questions You Must Answer Before You Die
15. Suffer No More
16. Success Is not Happiness, Happiness Is Success
17. God = Happiness

18. Life! Realized!!
19. True Love Is Bliss, Not Just a Kiss
20. True Meaning of Yoga
21. The Ultimate Goal of Life, MEN: Moksha, Enlightenment, Nirvana
22. Religion! A Kindergarten to Spirituality
23. Why Bad Things Can't Happen to Good People!
24. LIFE Is...Liberation from Ignorance and Finding True Enlightenment
25. The Ladder to Heaven
26. FEAR: False Expectations Appearing Real
27. Soul: We Don't Have a Soul, We Are the Soul!
28. But We Pray
29. EGOD: Let Go of Your Ego and You Will Find God
30. 100 Diamond Quotes
31. Life Manual
32. Peace
33. SatChitAnanda
34. Neti Neti Tat Twam Asi
35. The Law of AttrACTION
36. Satyam Shivam Sundaram
37. My Enlightenment Lifebook
38. When You Overcome the Fear of Death, You Start to Live
39. World Peace! A Simple Solution
40. Many Problems, One Solution
41. Live Life, Moment by Moment
42. The Spiritual Jigsaw Puzzle
43. The 4 Quarters of Life
44. Rebirth

45. How to Live a Spiritual Life in a Material World?
46. Life Is Karma
47. Poems for Life: Peace, Love, Bliss, Enlightenment and Eternal Happiness
48. Enlightenment: The Myth and the Truth
49. God Is Not God, God Is SIP
50. The 10 Commandments of Detached Attachment
51. Prema Yoga: The Yoga of Divine Love
52. Give, Before You Are Gone!
53. Mukti: Freedom
54. Stop It, Stupid! Discover the Mantra of Happiness
55. Don't Cut Your Cake! Awake! Your Birthday Is Fake
56. Realizations of a Yogi
57. Flip Over from Mind to Consciousness
58. Happiness Is Success
59. POSIEMOM: Particle of SIP, the Supreme Immortal Power in Every Molecule of Matter
60. A to Z of Death
61. A Treasure of Quotes
62. Shivoham
63. Conversations on Life with AiR
64. What Are You Going to DO with 'Today'?
65. I am a Soul, Soul Is SIP, I Am SIP, SIP Is in All
66. Spirituality for Children
67. The A to Z of Happiness
68. 8 Stages of Spiritual Awakening
69. Our Greatest Sin
70. Start a Quest to Discover the Purpose of Life
71. How to Overcome Fear, Worry, Stress, Anxiety & Depression

72. Dream vs Reality: Both Are Illusions
73. God-Realization
74. Can I Change My Life?
75. World's 50 Greatest Secrets
76. From Yoga to Moksha
77. Enlightened Ego
78. My Journey of Spiritual Awakening
79. How to Live with Peace, Love and Bliss
80. Discover the AiR Happpiness Secret
81. Spiritual Initiation and How to Self-Certify that You Are Enlightened
82. True Love
83. The 24 Roadblocks to Enlightenment
84. How to Live Life
85. The Way to Moksha Through Sanatana Dharma
86. Unhappiness is a Choice